# SAINT AUGUSTINE'S

## *Sin*

# GARRY WILLS

# SAINT AUGUSTINE'S
## *Sin*

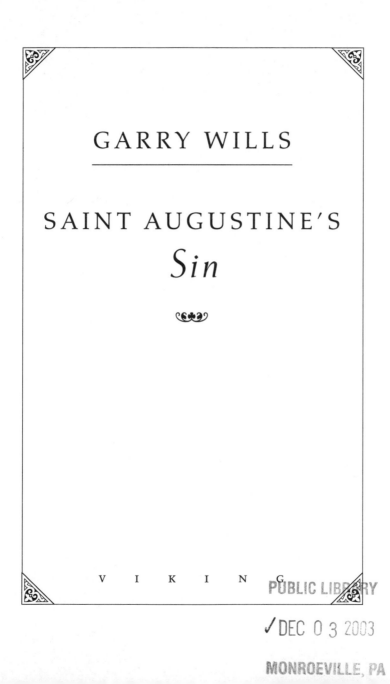

V I K I N G

VIKING
Published by the Penguin Group
Penguin Group (USA) Inc., 375 Hudson Street, New York, New York 10014, U.S.A.
Penguin Books Ltd, 80 Strand, London WC2R 0RL, England
Penguin Books Australia Ltd, 250 Camberwell Road, Camberwell, Victoria 3124,
   Australia
Penguin Books Canada Ltd, 10 Alcorn Avenue, Toronto, Ontario, Canada M4V 3B2
Penguin Books India (P) Ltd, 11 Community Centre, Panchsheel Park, New Delhi –
   110 017, India
Penguin Books (N.Z.) Ltd, Cnr Rosedale and Airborne Roads, Albany, Auckland,
   New Zealand
Penguin Books (South Africa) (Pty) Ltd, 24 Sturdee Avenue, Rosebank,
   Johannesburg 2196, South Africa

Penguin Books Ltd, Registered Offices: 80 Strand, London WC2R 0RL, England

First published in 2003 by Viking Penguin, a member of Penguin Group (USA) Inc.

10  9  8  7  6  5  4  3  2  1

LIBRARY OF CONGRESS CATALOGING-IN-PUBLICATION DATA

Augustine, Saint, Bishop of Hippo.
   [Confessiones. Liber 2. English]
   Saint Augustine's sin / [introduction and commentary by] Garry Wills.
      p. cm. — (Confessiones ; bk. 3)
   Includes bibliographical references.
   ISBN 0-670-03241-7 (alk. paper)
   1. Augustine, Saint, Bishop of Hippo.   2. Christian saints—Algeria—Hippo (Extinct
city)—Biography.   I. Wills, Garry, 1934–   II. Title.
BR65.A6E54 2003
270.2'092—dc21      2003043088
[B]

This book is printed on acid-free paper.  ∞

Printed in the United States of America
*Set in Aldus with Phaistos display and MT Arabesque Ornaments*
*Designed by Carla Bolte*

TO PETER BROWN

*who brought us Augustine*

# CONTENTS

# Key to Brief Citations

Boldface numerals in square brackets **[8]** refer to paragraphs in Book Two of *The Testimony*.

*comm.* refers to the Commentary on Book Two (p. 61).

O, with volume and page (e.g., O 2.52–53), refers to James J. O'Donnell, *Augustine, "Confessions"* (Oxford University Press, 1992).

T, with book and paragraph number (e.g., T 10.5), refers to books of *The Testimony* other than Book Two.

I translate all Scripture texts from the Latin versions Augustine used. The Psalms are numbered as in the Vulgate Latin Bible and in the Douay-Rheims Catholic translation of them.

# FOREWORD

In Book One of *The Testimony*, Augustine described his infancy and boyhood, when the effects of original sin were manifested in tendencies toward pride and other vices. In Book Two, he reaches an age (sixteen) when he is capable of deliberate sin—the *decision* to do wrong. He finds this mysterious power most obvious in the malice of an apparent *act gratuit*, the theft and destruction of useless pears. His surprising emphasis on this apparently trivial matter comes from its usefulness as a laboratory sample. It can be tested for what Augustine thought of as the emptiness of the evil act, its non-being. This connects the act with the three scriptural sins that were for Augustine the "founding sins," the original and "pure" acts of malevolence: the fallen angels' rebellion, Adam's fall, and Cain's sin as the founder of the City of Man. His own petty sin is read in the light of the scriptural descriptions of these great sins. None of those sins, it should be noticed, has anything to do with sexual transgressions, the thing that comes to people's minds all too readily when Augustine's sins are mentioned. I append to this book, therefore, Augustine's analysis of each of the three great sins.

# SAINT AUGUSTINE'S

## *Sin*

❦

# PART I

# Introduction

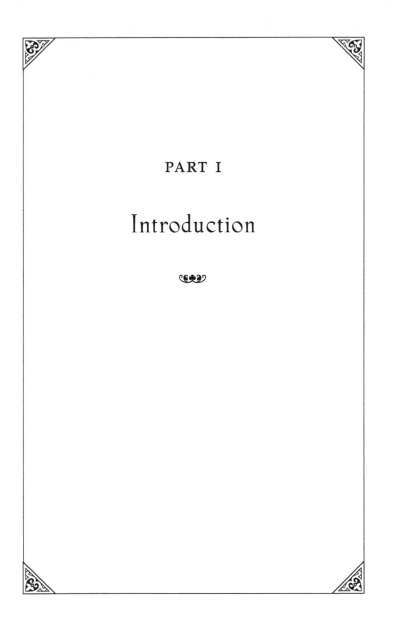

Augustine + sin = sex. That is the equation most people begin with when they first think of Augustine's *Testimony*. They are so obsessed with the idea that Augustine was obsessed with sex that they find it hard to read what he actually wrote about sin. He felt that he had committed far graver sins than those of the flesh. Few believe that he actually meant it when he said that his great sin at the age of sixteen (when he had probably already met and had sex with the mother of his child) was the theft of some pears. Many get around their own problem by trying to find a sexual meaning in that theft. If they cannot do that, they cannot take the man seriously when he speaks of sin. As Nietzsche wrote to his friend Overbeck:

> For a diversion I was just reading the *Confessions* of Saint Augustine, with great regret that you were not here with me. What a high-flown wordsmith! Such tear-jerking phoniness! How hard I laughed, for example, over a "pear theft" of his youth, made the basis for his account of student days (o 2.227).

Audiences come to hear the bishop talk about sex, and are not going to put up with anything so beside the point as agonies of regret over pears that were not edible anyway. Yet James O'Donnell (2.141) notes that "The meditation on the pear theft is the longest sustained passage on any topic so far in [the book]."

Worse in a way, is to come. The next long episode-cum-analysis—in Book Four of *The Testimony*—describes another sin. This one fits so little modern expectations that most readers miss the fact that it *is* the story of a sin—unless, of course, they can slip a sexual content into it (as Rebecca West did in her book on Augustine). The ordinary reader thinks it describes not a sin but a sorrow, a rather hysterical reaction to the death of a friend. Even so nonordinary a reader as Nietzsche found this the second-most absurd passage in the book:

> How psychologically phony (for example, when he relates the death of a friend with whom he made up one soul, and decided to live on, since in this way his friend would not be entirely dead.) What revolting pretentiousness.[1]

But if Augustine seems to exaggerate his other sins in a semi-hysterical way, he is equally guilty of exaggerating his sexual sins. Despite his reputation as a dissolute young man, he lived from age sixteen or seventeen to age thirty-one or thirty-two "faithful to one woman's bed" (T 4.1), a woman with whom he brought up their child in an exemplary way. Though the woman was not his wife, such common-law marriages were recognized not only by Roman law in Augustine's time but by the church itself, which formally sanctioned them in Canon 17 of the Council of Toledo (400 C.E.). Augustine's own mother seems to have got along well with her grandson and the boy's mother—she lived with the young parents, and her only recorded objection was not to the house's sleeping arrangements but to the Manichaeism her son was professing at the time (T 1.19).

Actually, Monnica did not want her son to marry—not, that is, until he had reached a stage in his career when he could marry "up" in terms of wealth and status. The family had invested a great deal in Augustine's career, and it wanted a return on the investment.[2] When the time came to arrange a marriage, Monnica, as executor of her husband's estate, chose the appropriate heiress. The girl was not yet of marriageable age (fifteen), so Augustine took an interim mistress—the only other woman we can be sure he ever slept with. It is to be noticed that, here again, he did not resort to promiscuity but to another stable relationship with one woman. Before his fiancée could become his betrothed, Augustine had returned to the faith of his youth and renounced the world. It was allowed him as a Christian to marry. But the rules for a truly observant Christian were, in that ascetical period, that sex should be indulged in marriage only as needed for procreation, and he thought it would be easier for him to abstain entirely than to face the trial of infrequent sex with a wife in the same bed with him [3]. There was little in this sexual history to discredit anyone but a man with the high standards of a saint. He had used the mother of his son disreputably, as he came to realize and admit (*What Good There Is in Marriage* 5.5). But he cannot reasonably be considered profligate.

Well, if his sex life was so respectable, what is all the fuss about? First of all, we must remember that the fuss is made mainly by modern readers, not by Augustine himself. For a man supposedly obsessed with sex, Augustine spent very little time on the sins of the flesh in his sermons. He warned his flock more about stinginess toward the poor and pride in their worldly possessions or status. Lack of sexual control was a result of original sin, not the cause of it, and it was not even the most signal part of that legacy. As the great Augustine scholar, Peter Brown, noted:

> Other signs of Adam's fall invariably struck Augustine, in his later years, as playing a far more powerful role in human affairs. The terrible cascade of helpless misery, of ignorance, arrogance, malice and violence set up a deafening roar. Beside these devastating ills, sexual temptation was no more than an irritating trickle. . . . In a standard edition [of *The City of God*], out of sixteen lines devoted to deliberate human sins, only two refer to sexuality.[3]

It is true that most of the material used to show that Augustine was obsessed with sex comes from those very "late years" Brown is describing; but that had to do with an accident of his controversy with the Pelagians.

If Augustine spends little time analyzing sexual sin, it is because there is little to analyze. There is no mystery to the appeal of pleasure. The surrender to it is a weakness but not, in itself, one of malice. It is not a mark of the great sinners, the cold rejectors of God, beginning with Satan. It is not a sin of pride, avarice, or tyranny. It was not the sin of Adam or of Eve. Sins of the spirit concerned him more than sins of the flesh. The latter he calls obvious, however reprobate, in their appeal: "[W]e sway to what touches the flesh or affects any of the senses by its fitness to them" **[10]**, "[l]imbs that intermingle in embrace" (T 10.8). Yielding to pleasure is thus understandable. He is harsher on those who actually seek pain, in the "transgressive knowledge" of sadomasochism (T 10.55). This comes closer to the desire for knowing and experiencing everything that Satan stands for. The two great sins of Augustine's youth—the pear theft and his reaction to the dying friend—resemble this transgressive knowledge more than they do any simple yielding to pleasure.

## 1. Adam's Sin

Just when, in *The Testimony*, Augustine has reached the age of sixteen and begun his active sexual life, he disappoints those who want the lurid details by devoting half of the book to a theft he and his fellow delinquents committed in a mangy orchard. Some try to ease their letdown by teasing some covert sexual meaning out of the pears. But that runs up against Augustine's claim that the whole basis for his bewilderment was the *lack* of sensual or other incitement to the crime [10–13]. If he were trying to enjoy something so obvious as sexual pleasure, there would be no mystery to the matter. Augustine is as emphatic as he can be on the *lack* of allurement in the pears or in the act of taking them. That is what bothers him. Why perform a malicious act, something harmful to others and not helpful to oneself, for the pure mischief of it? "Pure" mischief is the realm of Satan, not of sex-befuddled human beings. Augustine eliminates the obvious explanations in a very systematic way, like a detective crossing off suspects one by one.

In **[10]**, he crosses off any direct appeal the theft might have made to the senses, or to a desire for worldly power. In **[11]**, he distinguishes the motive for the act from motives for other crimes: sexual jealousy, desire for wealth or for the bare necessities of life, fear, revenge. In **[12]**, the act is denied any form of beauty—he goes through the entire scale of beings, eliminating moral beauty, human or animal beauty, inanimate beauty (including that involving any of the four elements). In **[13]**, he says that this theft did not even put up a pretense of right, as many crimes do—he lists fourteen of these virtue-pretending vices: pride, desire for glory, aggression, sensual indulgence, transgressive knowledge, willful ignorance, sloth, self-pampering, wastefulness, stinginess, envy, anger, cowardice, and melancholy. The robbery dispenses even with these masks. It is nakedly, unapologetically, wrong.

Then what can explain his own act to his own self? As usual, Augustine resorts to reflection on classical thought and scriptural imagery. The classical thought is contained in *Catiline's War* by Sallust and *Friendship* by Cicero. The scriptural text is that of Adam's fall in Genesis.

The story of Catiline's attempted coup d'état, thwarted by Cicero during his year as consul (63 B.C.E.), was famous not only from Cicero's four orations against the conspiracy, but from a historical monograph on the subject published by Sallust (Gaius Sallustius Crispus) two decades after the conspiracy was put down. (On Augustine's admiration for Sallust see, *comm.* [9].) Catiline is supposed to have augmented his revolutionary forces with youth gangs recruited on the streets to perform mischievous acts. These bands offer an obvious comparison with Augustine's raiders on the pear orchard, and he is thinking of them even before he expressly refers to Catiline in [11]. In [2], he says his sole delight was in "loving and being loved" *(amare et amari)*. Cicero in his second speech against Catiline (2.23), says of the man's young rioters: "These smooth pretty-boys were versed not only in loving and being loved [*amare et amari*], or singing and dancing, but in lunging with rapiers and dosing with poisons." Referring to himself and his cronies in [9], Augustine uses the dismissive diminutive *adulescentuli* ("young-menlings"). That there is a sneer in the term is seen from the Catilinarian invective Augustine refers to. It is not enough to translate the word, in those places, by a neutral English diminutive like "lads" or "striplings." It means "young punks." Here is the vituperative Cicero: "Is there any young punk [*adulescentulo*], provoked by your enticements [*inlecebris*] of the gutter, whom you [Catiline] have not marshaled with your sword toward aggression or with your torch toward dissipation?" (*Against Catiline* 1.13). Cato, in Sallust's account of Catiline's conspiracy, demands the death penalty for Catiline's young followers, dismissing calls for clemency: "Pardon them, indeed, as if the young punks [*adulescentuli*] were just led astray by ambition!" (*Catiline's War* 52.26).[4] That Augustine had Cicero's passage in mind, as well as that of Sallust, probably explains the use in the preceding sentence of *inlece-brosis* (not-enticing).

Sallust was useful to Augustine not just for the general comparison with young troublemakers but because Sallust expressly says that they acted without motive, as Augustine thinks for a while that he has done. "If no motive were at hand for doing wrong, he [Catiline] had his gang attack and murder innocent as well as guilty passersby . . ." (*Catiline's War* 16.3). But this, too, must be crossed off as an explanation for Augustine's act, since Sallust goes on immediately to *give* a motive even while repeating that there was none: "to keep their hands or hearts from losing edge for lack of practice, he was bad and brutal without motive." Catiline was toughening his little criminals to bigger tasks by getting them to indulge in minor gestures of aggression. Since Augustine and his fellow punks were not put up to their action by a mastermind plotting to overthrow the state, the Catiline parallel seems to have its limits. Cicero and Scripture will be more useful.

Having stripped away all apparent motive for the theft, Augustine tries to isolate its peculiar character by noting that he would not have robbed the orchard if he had been acting on his own. His itch to do the deed "required friction with colluding fellows to make it catch fire" **[16]**. So there *was* an apparent (deceptive) good in the act—the good of companionship. However hollow this claim to a good, it was enough to make the difference between solitary inaction and joint action. This was a crucially important point to Augustine, since he had taken years to escape the Manichaean claim that one can act on a directly evil motive. For that sect, there was a coordinate principle of evil operating in the world, along with and against God. Augustine rejected that notion when he reached the conclusion that there is no positive evil thing that can oppose God, the creator of everything that exists. Sin is an introduction of nonbeing into the created order by the will's abandonment of greater goods to slide down toward lesser ones, those with less existence where there should have been more. This is exemplified in the sin of the fallen angels. Their being remains a good thing, to the extent that they remain in existence; but that residue of good becomes itself a torture for the angels, precisely because it is a trace of the far greater good they lost when they abandoned God.

Companionship in evil is treated as a distortion and denial of real friendship in Cicero's dialogue, *Friendship*. Political friendship is the principal concern of Cicero, and he remarks of conspiracies against the state: "Without associates no one undertakes such things" (42). This is remarkably like Augustine's statement that he would not have raided the orchard all alone. And Cicero warns against the communal friction that ignites a desire for wrong: "Thus it is a maxim for the good that they must not consider themselves so implicated [*alligatos*] with friends that they cannot disengage from them when they are doing their country some great wrong" (42).

> Let this be the mandate of true friendship, that we neither request of another that they perform an unworthy act, nor accede to another issuing such a request. For it is an unworthy

defense, and by no means admissible, to say that we performed any evil act to please a friend, much less one against our own country (40).

Cicero repeatedly drives home the point that companionship in evil is no alleviation of the evil: "Nature grants friendship as a minister to the better, not a crony in the baser, conduct" (82). He makes the same point in the book of advice to his son (*Duty* 3.43): "If we were obliged to do anything [even wrong] that a friend wanted us to do, that would not be a friendship but a criminal cabal."

Useful as Cicero was to Augustine in helping him find a meaning in his "meaningless" act, a higher authority gave him the theological insight that was essential to his own tale of grace rejected and then restored. For him the greatest sin caused by a false ideal of companionship was Adam's. It is a vulgar misconception that Augustine traced the first man's original sin to sex. Adam's fall was due to a misplaced chivalry. Eve was misled by the serpent, supposing the godlike powers he offered to be real, but Augustine considered the First Letter to Timothy an authentically Pauline text, and it said (2.14): "Adam was not misled, though his wife was misled by the lie." Adam made a deliberate choice, out of his solidarity with Eve. In *First Meanings in Genesis* (11.59), which he began while working on *The Testimony*, Augustine wrote:

> After Eve had been deceived into eating of the forbidden tree, and offered him its fruit to eat along with her, Adam did not want to dismay her, since he thought she might be crushed,

without him to support her, if she were banished from his heart, to die from that separation. He was not overcome by disordered desire of the flesh, which he had not yet experienced as a disposition in his members at odds with his mind, but by a kind of friendly well-wishing [*amicalis quadam benevolentia*], which often makes us sin against God rather than turn a friend into a foe.

Later, in *The City of God* (14.11), Augustine gave the same interpretation to Adam's fall, even using the same parallel (how Solomon had joined in idol worship rather than offend his wives, 3 Kings 11.4):

Adam yielded to Eve in breaking God's law, not because he believed she was telling the truth, but out of a compulsion to solidarity [with her], as male to female, lone existing man to lone existing woman, human being to fellow human being, husband to wife. . . . [H]e refused to be rent from this special partnership [*unicum consortium*], even at the cost of joining her in sin. . . . In one way, however, he may have been misled: since he had no prior experience of God's rigor, he may have made light of the offense and, without being misled precisely as his wife had been, he too was fooled, by himself, when he expected his plea to work, that 'The wife you gave me was the one who gave me the fruit that I ate.' We need nothing more to conclude that, though they were not misled together by the same error, they were convicted together in sin, tangled up together in the devil's net.

In *Paradise Lost* (9.938–40, 952–59), Milton took Adam's fall straight from Augustine:

> Nor can I think that God, Creator wise,
> Though threat'ning, will in earnest so destroy
> Us, his prime creatures, dignified so high . . .
> However, I with thee have fix'd my lot,
> Certain to undergo like doom—if death
> Consort with thee, death is to me as life,
> So forcible within my heart I feel
> The bond of nature draw me to my own,
> My own in thee. For what thou art is mine,
> Our state cannot be severed. We are one,
> One flesh, to lose thee were to lose myself.

Milton's "bond of nature" is Augustine's "compulsion to solidarity" *(socialis necessitudo)*.

The sentimental modern reader may admire Adam's love and think "the world well lost" for such a primal loyalty. But the parallel here is Cicero's citizen committing treason for a friend. Adam had a *political* duty to the fate of mankind. It is not only his own death that is at stake but the blighted heritage he will leave behind. Because, in the scheme Augustine inherited, sin descends from the man, Adam cannot rescue Eve from her death but he can condemn everyone else to it. Since human solidarity is with Adam in the sexist theology Augustine shared with Paul and others, mankind would not have become mortal if Adam had not eaten the fruit. Because he would not struggle with the compulsion to solidarity, nor trust God and consult him, he proved a traitor to his duty—just as Solomon was when he imported the political evil of idolatry into his nation for the sake of another *socialis necessitudo.*

Why does Augustine find a deadly meaning in anything so trivial as the pear theft? Eating the fruit in Eden looked trivial, too. The gravity is not measured by the pettiness of the thing prohibited but by the immensity of the God who prohibits. "Robbery is undeniably punished by your law, but also by the law written in men's hearts, which not even their own evil can efface—for what robber will calmly submit to being robbed?" **[9]**. Was Augustine thinking of Adam's sin as he reflected on his own sin? How could he not be? Both involve a theft of fruit; both are performed because of an associative tie. Adam refused to be detached from his "special partnership" *(unicum consortium)*. Augustine "must have loved a partnership [*consortium*] with my fellows in the theft. . . . [W]hat I wanted was to commit the crime in partnership [*consortium*] with those sharing my sin" **[16]**. To underline the parallel with Adam's sin, Augustine refers to "the pear tree" (singular), though he and his fellows took huge loads *(onera ingentia)* of fruit from the orchard **[9]**.

The sin of the theft fascinates Augustine because it is so striking a reenactment of Adam's sin. He was not driven to it by mere sensual urges or conventional utility. Though there is no such thing as pure evil, this was as close to a purely evil choice as he was likely to reach. And perhaps it was not, after all, very far from the crimes of Catiline's gang. The punks of

Rome were put up to minor mischief by their leader, who had larger conspiratorial aims. With the pears Augustine, like Adam, was falling into the devil's trap of thinking a minor rebellion against God trivial because the stolen things were inconsiderable. But God is not inconsiderable. By treating him as such, Adam made a calculated choice, not a mere blind lunge of lust. Of course, the sin of Adam can never be replicated—he made a sinful choice without already having suffered the consequences of sin. That is what gives his sin a certain clarity. For men and women after him, each sin is also and already a punishment for sin, made under the hobbling circumstances of mankind's fallen condition.

> [But] Adam, when he sinned, had absolutely nothing evil in him pressuring him, against his own resistance, to do wrong, nothing to make him say [with Paul] "I do not the good I would; rather, the evil I would not, I do" (Romans 7.19). . . . From this you can distinguish three different things, and identify them as: sin, the punishment for sin, and the combination of the two (*Unfinished Answer to Julian* 2.47).

Adam's sin was what might be called pure sin, uncontaminated with the effects of prior sin. Death and ignorance are examples of sin's punishment that are not sins in themselves. And all our own sins are the product of the third condition, the combination of actual sin and the punishment of earlier sin affecting the new one. The pear theft was, then, an example of this third or combined condition.

It is striking, for all that, how close Augustine came, even in his fallen condition, to replicating Adam's fall. The points of similarity are (a) an apparently trivial matter, which nonetheless (b) was clearly forbidden by God, and with (c) none of the more obvious passions driving him or clear rewards drawing him—with, in fact, nothing but (d) the associative tie with others as a motive. Now we can see why Augustine took such an exhaustive approach to the refining process by which he boiled down motives and rewards, eliminating all "impurities," to reach the minimum remaining reason for his act, the *socialis necessitudo*. Only by that process could he study, as in a laboratory experiment, the nature of sin in itself, somewhat as Adam experienced it.

And it is essential to his purpose that his sin, like Adam's, have no hint of sexual hedonism in its motivation. In *First Meanings in Genesis*, Augustine says Adam did not make his choice "overcome by disordered desire of the flesh, which he had not yet experienced as a disposition in his members at odds with his mind." This is a quotation from Romans 7.23: "I see another disposition in my members, at odds with my mind's disposition." Paul is describing the *result* of Adam's sin, not its *cause*. Lack of sexual control became a sign of the loss of integrity that followed on Adam's rebellion against God. Sexual intercourse, Augustine taught, would have occurred in Eden, but without the drivenness of the postlapsarian disposition. There would have been sex, but no rape. All intercourse would have been fully consensual and without shame. The woman would not have the impediment of a hymen, and parturition would have been unobstructed:

Of course there would have been conjugal relations, even if original sin had not been committed—otherwise why was Adam given a woman as his helper, instead of man? God's command, 'Increase and multiply,' was not a forecast of sins deserving damnation but a blessing upon married fertility. . . . But there would have been no pain or blood on a virgin's first experience of sex, and there would have been no shriek of a woman in childbirth (*Christ's Grace and Original Sin* 2.40).

Natural and innocent intercourse of sexual partners would have occurred in Eden, even without commission of any sin, for children can be born in no other way, to fulfill God's blessing ["Increase . . ."]. . . . But the sexual drive would not have put man to the test against his own will, nor have compelled the chastity of a woman if she resisted (*Unfinished Answer to Julian* 5.16).

Adam forfeited perfect freedom of choice, in this as in other areas, by his choice of the less-existent good in Eden. As his will rebelled against God, his body now rebels against his will. There is a disconnect between human components, the body not submitting to the will. This is shown as much by impotence as by concupiscence:

At times, unsignaled by the will, the body stirs on its own, insistent; while at other times it will not respond to a lover's grunts. In the mind, all is flaming—all freezing in the body; so that, odd as it may seem, even where sex for pleasure and not for procreation is concerned, lust can leave lust in the lurch [*libidini libido non servit*]. Though lust normally fights the mind's controls, sometimes it is in civil strife with itself, and even after provoking a riot in the mind, it cannot maintain itself by making riot in the body (*The City of God* 14.15).

Augustine the satirist makes fun of the impotent lover's plight. The mind-body inconcinnity is rhetorically marked by chiasmus (the a-b-b-a order): "Mind-flaming//freezing-body" *(in animo ferveat, friget in corpore)*. The last sentence above has a sunken political imagery—the story of a fizzled coup d'état, as of a Catiline unable to keep his own troops stirred up.

So Augustine, in order to understand the nature of sin, goes back before the consequence of sin to find the way he came closest to sharing the sin of Adam. Only by understanding his solidarity with Adam can he appreciate his redemption in solidarity with Christ. While others want him to provide them with a psychology of sex, he is more interested in the theology of sin.

## 2. Book Two, Organizing Principles

*The Testimony* is built up on layers of theological symbols. The early books are organized around the six ages of man, which in turn call up their complements, the six ages of history and the six days of creation. The first age was marked at T 1.7, the second at T 1.13. The fourth will be reached at T 7.1. Book Two opens with the announcement that Augustine has reached the third age, *adulescentia*, which runs from puberty all the way to age thirty (and is not, therefore, "adolescence" in our sense, but young manhood). To see how rich this scheme was in Augustine's hand, a chart will be helpful:

| Ages of Man | Six Days | History |
|---|---|---|
| 1. *Infantia* (pre-verbal) | Light | Adam to Noah |
| 2. *Pueritia* (speaking) | Sky/Earth | Noah to Abraham |
| 3. *Adulescentia* (15-30) | Waters/Plants | Abraham to David |
| 4. *Juventus* (30-45) | Planets | David to Babylon |
| 5. *Maturitas* (45-60) | Fish | Babylon to Christ |
| 6. *Senectus* (60-90) | Animals/Man | Christ to End |

In exploring his own "third age," Augustine uses the days of creation and the ages of history to understand what he was going through. On the third day, the waters were gathered together and defined by separation from land, and vegetation was sown on earth. In the third age, the principal event was the wandering through the desert, with infidelity committed along the way, but merciful conduct leading the chosen home. For Augustine, the scriptural Exodus always called up the parable of the prodigal son, who wandered before returning to his father. To take separately the items in this cluster of concepts and images, consider (a) the vegetation, (b) the gathered and limited waters, and (c) the Prodigal.

*Vegetation.* Since the principal subject in this book is going to be Augustine's pear tree reflecting Adam's tree, the misuse of vegetation is important throughout the book—not only Adam's eating of a tree's produce, but his flight into trees' shadow and his attempt to cover his nudity with leaves. The text of Genesis 1.9 in the Latin used by Augustine ran this way:

> And God said, "Let earth bear plants of foison, each seeding its own kind to its own likeness, the fruit tree bearing fruit of its own kind and its own likeness across the earth."5 And it was done—the earth bore plants of foison, each seeding its own kind to its own likeness, the fruit tree bearing fruit of its own kind to its own likeness across the earth. And God saw it, a good thing. And night came, then day—it was the third day.

The only plant singled out for specific mention is the fruit tree, a foreshadowing of the importance of Adam's tree.

In the first paragraph of Book Two, Augustine's maturing body is seen in terms of vegetal lushness: "At the time of my young manhood, when I burned to be engorged with vile things [like Adam eating the fruit of the tree], I boldly foisoned into ramifying and umbrageous loves. . . ." He uses the rare verb "to forest out" *(silvescere)* with its rarer metaphorical sense. I use a comparably rare verb for lush growth, "to foison." His umbrageous *(umbrosis)* growth is dark, like the shade Adam seeks after his sin: "He fled toward an umbrous place [*ad umbram*] and hid amid the trees of Paradise" (*Explaining the Psalms* 37.15).

The vegetal images continue. He does not let God's grace soften "the thorns not allowed to grow in Eden" **[3]**. When he resists God, "my heart's gardener" [5], "the thorns of my own drives, with no one to weed them out from around me, shot up above my head" [6]. He sought shadow that "sealed me off from the serenity of your truth" [8]. Sins that try to hide their real nature are "shadowy" (*umbratica,* [12]). His own so-called freedom is a shadowy *(tenebrosa)* pretense [14]. His apparent lushness hides an inner "withering" [1], one that makes him a barren "terrain of deprivation" [18].

*Waters gathered and defined.* On the third day of creation, before vegetation was bid to grow on the land, an earlier work had to occur:

> And God said, "Let the water under heaven be united into a single union so that dry land rise." And it was done. The water under heaven was united into a single union, and earth appeared. And God called the dry land "earth," and the union of water "sea."

In his own third age, Augustine sees himself as dissolute, as liquid and loose, a stormy surge not confined by boundaries. Water is the lowest of the four elements. Augustine calls it the element "nearest formlessness . . . unfixed in its flowing quality" (*First Meanings in Genesis* 2.11). Augustine himself is like the waters before the Spirit hovered over them, an unformed chaos. To suggest his own condition, Augustine creates a chaotic sentence, all formless surge and reflux upon itself, one whose only stability is provided by reference to the boundaries that *are not there:*

I did not observe the line where mind meets mind. Instead of affection's landmarks drawn in light, earthmurks drowned in lust—and my erupting sexuality—breathed mephitic vapors over the boundary, to cloud and blind my heart in clouds and fog, erasing the difference between love's quietness and the drivenness of dark impulse. Quietness and drives were mingled chaotically within me, battering my impotent maturity on the anfractuosities of desire and dousing me in a maelstrom of offenses [2].

The interchangeability of everything here is suggested by the complex wordplay between *limes* (landmark) and *limosa* (earthmurky)—both have the same etymology, from *limus* (our "loam"), but one refers to markings on dry land and the other to sinkings in wet land. This etymological wordplay is crossed by the sound-play of *luminosa* ("drawn in light") and *limosa*. Light almost *becomes* dark in this clustering of near-samenesses and near-opposites, entangled in alliterations and assonances.

The ungathered waters of Augustine were also referred to in Book One, where the *shaping* waters of baptism were denied him. Those would have formed his clay, as the waters are separated from dry land on the third day:

Mighty storm-waves, and many, were foreseen rolling over me after my childhood; and my mother, understanding this, preferred to commit to the waters' workings my unshaped clay, rather than a self already reshaped (T 1.18).

In *Testimony* Book Two, the separation of water from earth on the third day calls to Augustine's mind Job 38.10–11: "I set limits for the sea, clamped on its locks and doors, and said: 'Come thus far only, you will not cross over, your flood will break back upon itself.' " That is what, to his sorrow, did not happen to him in his fluidly dissolute youth:

> Who might have brought within boundaries my misery, turned to some purpose the evanescent beauties of extreme experience, and set a clear limit to their deliciousness, that the stormy waters of my youth might have seethed up only to the shoreline of marriage? [3].

The gathering in from dissipation that the third day stands for in Augustine's mind is a theme already sounded in the book's opening paragraph: "You gather me from my own scatterings, after I have torn myself from your unity and fallen into multiplicity." The water image is there again in [4]: "I frothed along in the wake of my driving passion."

There is an implicit reference to God's gathered waters in [6], at the public baths, where his father's scrutiny can see only earthly fertility, "clothed" in mortal nudity. This is in clear contrast to the scrutiny before baptism, when one is "clothed" in Christ. The waters of baptism are a *saving* flood.

*The Prodigal.* The rich opening paragraph of Book Two has suggestions of the prodigal son's departure and return—a pattern that has made some critics claim that the parable of Luke 15.11–32 is the armature around which the whole of

*The Testimony* is formed.[6] However exaggerated that may be, the Prodigal's tale is especially applicable to the book of Augustine's *adulescentia*, since the Prodigal was *adulescentior* (Luke 15.12), the *younger* brother. The Prodigal "longed to fill his belly with husks," just as Augustine—in the opening paragraph—"burned to be engorged with vile things." As the son "parted [*divisit*] the inheritance," destroying its unity, and "scattered out [*dissipavit*] his part," so Augustine is "torn [*discussus*] from your unity" to "fall into multiplicity." As the son "returned to himself," so God regathers Augustine from his self-dispersion *(a dispersione)*. The son confesses that "I have sinned before [*coram*] you," and Augustine admits that he was "decomposing before [*coram*] your eyes." All those echoes of the Prodigal's plight are in the short opening paragraph.

The Prodigal in Luke (15.13) "goes into a far-off [*longinquam*] country." Augustine, in Book Two, "wandered farther [*longius*] from you, as you played out the leash. . . . I ranged farther out [*porro longe*] from you" **[2]**. He "left you [God] to range beyond all the limits of your law, though not beyond your scourge's reach" **[4]**. Like the son whose father waits at home, he is " 'in distant [*longe*] exile from the comforts of your dwelling' " **[4]**. He is "on the crooked paths that men tread when 'going away from you, not toward you' "**[6]**.

When famine strikes the far-off country where the Prodigal is residing, he succumbs to deprivation (*egestas*, Luke 15.14). Augustine, in his wandering from God, makes of himself "a terrain of deprivation" (*regio egestatis*, **[18]**).

## 3. Translating Book Two

Augustine is a jazzy writer. His passages are one continual play of rhetorical pyrotechnics. So true is this that some critics, like Edward Gibbon, call his style "usually clouded by false and affected rhetoric."[7] But one would never know this from reading most translations. Their authors must have concluded that they could not or should not try to reproduce the continual wordplay, the acoustical effects, the intermeshing verbal arrangements. As a result they strip Augustine of what Gibbon found offensive, creating an intellectually "chaster" but emotionally more distant writer than one finds in the original Latin. This reduction may satisfy those who think rhetoric a matter of ornaments superadded to content. But Augustine clearly *thought* in terms of verbal matings, dancings, and duels. To wrench him free from those intellectual patterns is to lobotomize him.

Take a simple example. Here is a clause in **[9]**, as Englished by the respected translator Henry Chadwick: "Our pleasure lay in doing what was not allowed." That gives the "plain sense" of *eo liberet quo non liceret,* but it misses the lubricious *sound* of it, the way the verbs fold into each other with a serpentine sinuosity, *enacting* temptation. An English equivalent would be something like "Simply what was not allowed allured us." Or take *nimis inimica amicitia* **[17]**, which Chadwick interprets rather than translates as "Friendship can be a dangerous enemy," missing the etymological play, the tight paradoxical formulation, the assonance (adding with *nimis* two more *i*-sounds to the four already present), and the alliteration of NiMis with *iNiMica aMicitia*, as well as the revulsion being expressed toward something that is supposed to be pleasant. Something much stronger is called for: "How infectious, then, is this affection."

Augustine is often funny, in a satirical way. This is true not only in his spirited polemics with the heretical, but in the self-mockery of his own sinful contradictions: "[There was] I, loftily downfallen, actively paralyzed, sowing arid and ever more arid sadnesses" **[2]**. He turns satire on his father when he puns on *disertus* and *desertus* at **[5]**. His father wants him to be verbally deft; so he turns a verbal trick on him, playing on the sounds: "so long as I should be verbally fertile—futile, rather." This is rhetoric making fun of rhetoric, as in his other use of the same pun in *Explaining the Psalms* 36.3.6: "You understand us better when we blurt out our message than when, trying to be deft, we are bereft" *(disertudine . . . deserti)*.

I do not translate the pun as "deft . . . bereft" in **[5]** because it is embedded, there, in a long image having to do with the vegetation theme of the third day of creation: "[T]his father could not be bothered with my cultivation in your eyes, nor with my chastity, so long as I should become verbally fertile—futile, rather, without the tending you provide, God, my heart's gardener skilled and true." The agricultural terms are *crescerem . . . desertus . . . cultura . . . dominus agri*. To maintain this continuity of imagery, I transfer the vegetation sense from one word in the pun *(desertus)* to the other *(disertus)*. Augustine thought in terms of images, as Bible symbolism required.

Neglect of this, or of any of his rhetorical tools, deprives the reader of an essential part of the experience of watching his mind work. For bravura effects, like the description of watery chaos in [2] (see pages 33–35), the translator must search out as many cognate English effects as he can find.

## Notes to Introduction

1. Bertolt Brecht was no more impressed: "For want of trashy novels I read *The Confessions* of Augustine. . . . The typical attitude of intellectuals to their insights was so laughable—an attitude protective, hoarding, and, yes, gloating." O'Donnell, noting that Nietzsche read the book "for diversion" and Brecht for want of junk literature, says: "Perhaps German intellectuals should not take to the *Confessions* as light reading" (O 2.227).

2. Brent D. Shaw, "The Family in Late Antiquity," *Past and Present* 115 (1987), pp. 33–36.

3. Peter Brown, *The Body and Society* (Columbia University Press, 1988), p. 416.

4. The sneer in the term *adulescentulus* is obvious in some places outside the Catiline literature. The young Pompey, for instance, is called "a murderous young punk" *(adulescentulus carnifex)* in Valerius Maximus, *Deeds and Wonders* 6.2.8. Elsewhere, however, the term is neutral, as when Caesar writes, "Our men wanted to show what could be accomplished under a stripling's leadership." *(adulescentulo duce)*, *War in Gaul* 3.21.

5. "Plants of foison"—*herba pabuli*, where *pabulum* suggests lush growth and nourishment of all kinds.

6. Georg Nicolaus Knauer, "*Peregrinatio Animae*," *Hermes* 85 (1957), pp. 216–48.

7. Edward Gibbon, *The History of the Decline and Fall of the Roman Empire*, edited by J. B. Bury (Methuen & Co., 1909), p. 431.

# PART II

# The Testimony, Book Two

## Notes

L4 *toward you*] Reading *istuc*, not *istud* (O 2.105).

L5 *back up to expression*] *Re-cogitare:* Augustine explains the meaning of *cogito* at T 10.18, where he derives it from *cogo*, press together.

L7 *never deluding . . . ever delighting*] For the chiming effect of *dulcedo non fallax, dulcedo felix.*

L10 *young manhood*] See Introduction, page 20, on the sense of *adulescentia.*

L11 *boldly foisoned into ramifying*] Literally "was bold to forest out [*sil-vescere*] in different ways." See Introduction, page 21.

L11 *umbrageous loves*] For the shadow of trees as a place to hide in this book, see Introduction, page 21.

L12 *withering*] Daniel 10.8: "But my form was changed and I withered."

L14 *trying to please*] Psalm 52.6: "God has scattered the bones of those who are pleasing to men."

L15 *loving and being loved*] Cicero, *Against Catiline* 2.23: "These smooth pretty-boys were versed not only in loving and being loved . . ." (Introduction, page 9).

L16 *line where mind meets mind*] For *modus* as a defining boundary, see *comm.*

L17 *landmarks drawn in light . . . earthmurks drowned in lust*] For the play on *limes* and *limosa* (connected etymologically), as well as on *luminosa* and *limosa* (connected in sound). See Introduction, page 23.

L22 *impotent maturity*] A paradox—his apparent sexual fertility goes with a lack of real (spiritual) power.

# I. Sexual Offenses

1.  I am determined to bring back in memory the revolting things I did, and the way my soul was contaminated by my flesh—doing this not out of love for those deeds but as a step toward loving you. I move toward you this way because I would love to love you. I bring back up to expression the bitterness of my vile wanderings so you may sweeten them, you my sweetness never deluding, sure sweetness ever delighting. You gather me from my own scatterings, after I have torn myself from your unity and fallen apart into multiplicity. At the time of my young manhood, when I burned to be engorged with vile things, I boldly foisoned into ramifying and umbrageous loves, while my inner shapeliness was withering—I was decomposing before your eyes while in men's eyes I was pleasing myself and 'trying to please them.'

2.  Where did I find any satisfaction then but in loving and being loved? But I did not observe the line where mind meets mind. Instead of affection's landmarks drawn in light, earthmurks drowned in lust—and my erupting sexuality—breathed mephitic vapors over the boundary, to cloud and blind my heart in clouds and fog, erasing the difference between love's quietness and the drivenness of dark impulse. Quietness and drives were mingled chaotically within me, battering my impotent

L1 *dousing me in a maelstrom]*   Water imagery from the division of water from land in Genesis 1.9 (see Introduction, page 23).

L4 *wandered farther]*   Luke 15.13: "he wandered to a far-off land."

L5 *outflingings . . .]*   A list of spiritual deviations put in terms of the soul's physical "cosmology" *(comm.).*

L7 *slow to hear]*   See T 10.38: "Slow was I, Lord, too slow in loving . . ."

L8 *ranged farther out]*   Another reference to the prodigal son.

L8 *loftily downfallen . . . actively paralyzed]*   Three further paradoxes to suggest the cosmic jumble in his soul *(comm.).*

L10 *boundaries . . . limit . . . shoreline]*   Job 38.10–11: "I set limits for the sea, clamped on it locks and doors, and said: 'Come this far only, you will not cross over, your flood will break back upon itself.' " Introduction, page 24.

L17 *thorns not allowed to grow]*   Genesis 3.17–18: "He said to Adam: 'The earth will resist all your labors . . . it will bear you thorn and thistle . . .' " Part of the vegetation imagery of the third day of creation.

L20 *voice out of the clouds]*   Matthew 3.17: "a voice out of heaven saying."

L20 *They have all these cares]*   1 Corinthians 7.28: "They have all these cares of the flesh, which I would spare you."

L22 *Better for man]*   1 Corinthians 7.1: "Better for man not to lay hand to a woman."

L22 *man who has no wife]*   1 Corinthians 7.32–33: "The man who has no wife expresses concern for God, and wants to please him, while the man with a wife expresses concern for worldly matters, since he wants to please his wife."

L27 *castrated for heaven's reign]*   Matthew 19.12: "There are eunuchs who have castrated themselves for heaven's reign."

maturity on the anfractuosities of desire and dousing me in a maelstrom of offenses. Your ire impended over me, but I was unaware of it, deafened by the clattering of my mortal chains, a deafness inflicted by my soul's loftiness. I wandered farther from you, as you played out the leash—I was full of outfling- ings, effusions, diffusions, and ebullitions of illicit loves, as you maintained your silence. You, the joy I was so slow to hear, said nothing as I ranged farther out from you—I, loftily downfallen, actively paralyzed, sowing arid and ever more arid sadnesses.

3.   Who might have brought within boundaries my mis- ery, turned to some purpose the evanescent beauties of extreme experience, and set a clear limit to their deliciousness, that the stormy waters of my youth might have seethed up only to the shoreline of marriage? But could I have limited myself to sex used only for begetting children, Lord, as your law commands? (Yet it is you who make images of our mortality, able to soften with your gentling touch the thorns not allowed to grow in Eden, since your omnipotence is never far from us, however far from you we are.) In any case, I might have pondered more carefully your voice out of the clouds saying, 'They [the mar- ried] have all these cares of the flesh, which I would spare you.' Or 'Better for man not to lay hand to a woman,' or 'The man who has no wife expresses concern for God, and wants to please him, while the man with a wife expresses concern for worldly matters, because he wants to please his wife.' Had I listened to your words with greater attention, then with greater anticipa- tion I might have welcomed your embrace as one 'castrated for heaven's reign.'

L1 *frothed along in the wake*]    More sea imagery from Genesis 1.9.

L7 *affix your pain to precept*]    Psalm 93.20: "The seat of iniquity will never embrace you, who affix your pain to precept."

L8 *heal with a wound*]    Deuteronomy 32.39: "I will heal with a wound."

L8 *slay us*]    Deuteronomy 32.39: "I will slay in order to give life."

L10 *In distant exile*]    Micah 2.9: "You expelled the women from the dwelling of their comforts." The Prodigal's journey to "a far-off land" is also recalled.

L13 *cravings condoned . . . condemned*]    For the play on *libidines licentiosae . . . inlicitae*.

L27 *from what depths*]    Psalm 129.1: "From the depths I have cried up to you, Lord."

4.   Instead, I frothed along in the wake of my driving passion, having left you to range beyond all the limits of your law, though not beyond your scourge's reach—for who is beyond that? You had not in fact left me, but showed a pitying severity. You dashed with bitter repinings my forbidden joys, making me seek joys with no repining, which I would never find apart from you, Lord, apart from the way 'you affix your pain to precept,' and 'heal with a wound,' and 'slay us that we may not die' by loss of you.

Where did that leave me? 'In distant exile from the comforts of your dwelling' during this sixteenth year of my age, when I surrendered with ready hand all rule over my self, turning it over to mad cravings condoned by our debased humanity but condemned by your law. My family did not care to divert me from my mad course toward marriage. They cared only that I might acquire rhetoric and sway others with my words.

5.   It was in this sixteenth year that my studies were interrupted, when I was brought back from Madauros, the nearby town for which I had first left home in order to study grammar and rhetoric. My father was saving up funds to send me farther off, for study in Carthage, a project better suited to his aspirations than to his acquisitions, since he was a townsman of slender estate in Thagaste. Why do I bring this up? I do not bring it up to you, Lord, but in your presence I bring it up to my fellows, my fellow human beings—those, at any rate, however few, who may chance upon this book. And why to them? That we may express together, I and my readers, 'from what depths we must cry up to you' (though what could come closer to you

L1 *faithful life*]  Habakkuk 2.4: "The virtuous lead a faithful life."

L6 *my cultivation*]  *crescerem tibi,* a sounding of the vegetation theme, like "my heart's gardener" that follows.

L7 *fertile . . . futile*]  For the play on *disertus . . . desertus* (Introduction, page 27).

L16 *clothed* [indutum] *with unstable manhood*]  The imagery of clothing is a reference to a baptismal text, Romans 13.14: "Be clothed [*induite*] in Christ Jesus" *(comm.).*

L22 *your own temple*]  1 Corinthians 3.16: "See you not that you are God's own temple?"

L23 *your holy habitation*]  Ecclesiasticus 24.14: "I [Wisdom] maintain a holy habitation in his presence."

L24 *was jolted*]  Reading the rare and strong verb *exivilit* (literally, "jerked").

L25 *holy apprehension*]  2 Corinthians 7.15: ". . . how with apprehension and trembling you welcomed him."

L27 *away from you*]  Jeremiah 2.27: "They turned away from me, not toward me."

than the testifying heart and 'a faithful life'?). An instance is this man, my father, whom all were extolling since he squandered money beyond his means to finance his son's education in a distant place. Admittedly, many wealthier men made no such arrangement for their children, but this father could not be bothered with my cultivation in your eyes, nor with my chastity, so long as I should become verbally fertile—futile, rather, without the tending you provide, God, my heart's gardener skilled and true.

6.  So, in this my sixteenth year, in an idleness caused by my father's impecunious state, with no school to attend, I began again to stay with my parents, and the thorns of my own drives, with no one to weed them out from around me, shot up above my head. So much was this true that when my father saw in the baths that my childhood was gone and I was clothed with unstable young manhood, he mentioned this to my mother, overjoyed with anticipation of having grandchildren by me. It was the intoxicated joy with which the world forgets you the creator, to love in your place what you created, drunk on the invisible wine of desires deflected from you and declined toward the depths. But you had already begun to hallow 'your own temple' within my mother, laying the foundation for 'your holy habitation' there, while my father had only recently become a candidate for baptism. She was jolted 'with holy apprehension and trembling' that I, though also not baptized, would be set on the crooked paths that men tread when 'going away from you, not toward you.'

7.  Can I, alas, have the nerve to claim that you were saying

L12  *son of your servingwoman]*  Psalm 115.16: "O Lord, I am your servant, your servant and the son of your servingwoman."

L16  *orgasmic over orgies . . .]*  To represent the play on *libebat . . . libidine.*

L17  *vilification . . . villainy]*  To represent the play on *vituperatione nisi vitium* and *vituperarer vitiosior.*

L23  *in whose filth I wallowed]*  Jeremiah 38.22: "They have sunk your feet in filth and slime."

L23  *cinnamon and precious ointments]*  Song of Songs 4.14: "cinnamon . . . with all the finest ointments."

L25  *agglutinate]*  *haererem* with the filth *(caenum)* above.

L25  *to its underbelly]*  Ezekiel 38.12: "a dweller in earth's underbelly."

L27  *escaped from the center]*  Jeremiah 51.6: "escape from the center of Babylon."

nothing to me as I strayed from you? Were you in fact saying nothing at that time? Then whose if not yours were the words you drummed into my ears through my mother? But they did not sink into my heart, to make me act. She wished—and I recall deep within me how urgently insistent was she—that I would refrain from all illicit sex, but especially from relations with a married woman. Her warnings seemed old wives' tales to me, too embarrassing to be taken seriously. But these warnings came, without my knowing it, from you—I thought you were saying nothing, while what she said proved that you were not silent after all. It was you I scorned in scorning her—I her son, 'the son of your servingwoman, and myself your servant.' In my ignorance I blundered on, so blinded that it shamed me to be less shameless than my fellows. I listened as they boasted of their deeds, and the more perverse the deeds, the more pride they took in them, not only orgasmic over orgies but over publicizing them. What could more deserve vilification than such villainy? Yet I actually became villainous to *avoid* vilification— where I could not match them in admission of foul ways, I feigned deeds never done, preferring to be thought more outrageous than conformist, more dissolute than respectable.

8.    These, then, were the fellows I strolled about with on the streets of Babylon, in whose 'filth I wallowed' as if in 'cinnamon and precious ointments.' My invisible enemy was treading me down there, to agglutinate me 'to its underbelly,' taking in one who wanted the taking. The mother of my flesh, though she had 'escaped from the center of Babylon,' still lingered in its territory, and despite her advice to me on continence, in response

L14 *fattened*]    Psalm 72.7: "They have fattened as it were on evil."

to what she had heard from her husband, she did not try to check (if she could not repress) my pernicious and potentially fatal conduct. She did not try this because she feared that her ambitions for me would be thwarted by a wife. This had nothing to do with her ambition for my future life with you, but with the ambition she and her husband shared for my career in rhetoric, he because he thought nothing about you and nothing sensible about me, and she because she calculated that the traditional course of rhetoric would do me no harm in itself and might help me to serve you—or so I suppose, reading my parents' motives as well as I can. The reins were therefore loosed on me, to be tossed about, with no moderating discipline, by random influences. Deep fog sealed me off from the bright sun of your truth while I 'fattened as it were on my own evil.'

L1 *by your law]* Exodus 20.15: "Do no theft."

L2 *in men's hearts]* Romans 2.15: "Who show the effect of law written in their hearts." Jeremiah 31.33: "... promulgating in their hearts my laws, laws I will write on their hearts." (*Chiasmus* in original.)

L7 *bloated out]* Augustine is paradoxically "deprived" by being over-supplied with a bloat *(sagina)* of evil, leaving no room for what is right *(justitia)*. O'Donnell says the use of *sagina* is "designedly coarse" (O 2.129), and compares it with "fattened ... on my own evil" at **[8]**.

L10 *near our vineyard]* Augustine's father grew grapes, not pears. The "better" pears Augustine had at his disposal were probably those of his rich patron, Romanian.

L10 *not enticing* Unlike the fruit that tempted Eve at Genesis 3.6: "The woman saw that the tree was good for its fruit, and fair to the eye, and desirable."

L13 *malicious* [nequissimi] *young punks* [adulescentuli]] For the denigrative diminutive *adulescentuli,* borrowed from the denunciations of Catiline by Cicero and Sallust, see Introduction, page 9.

L16 *not allowed allured]* To repeat the chiming play on *liberet quo non liceret.*

L22 *my own lack]* For sin as non-being, see Appendix, page 76.

# II. Pear Theft

9. Robbery is undeniably punished by your law, but also by the law written in men's hearts, which not even their own evil can efface—for what robber will calmly submit to being robbed? Not even a wealthy robber will submit to one pressed by want. Yet I desired to commit robbery, and did it. I was driven by no deprivation—unless by a deprivation of what is right, a revulsion at it, while I was bloated out with evil. I stole things I had much more of, and much better. I wanted the stealing, not the thing stolen. I wanted the sin.

There was a pear tree near our vineyard, laden with fruit not enticing either in appearance or in taste. In dead night, after prolonging our pranks in the streets, as was our noxious custom, we malicious young punks steered our way to the tree, shook down its fruit and carted it off, a huge load we did not want to eat ourselves but to throw before swine—or if we ate some of it, that was not our motive. Simply what was not allowed allured us. Do you see into my heart, God, see a heart you can take pity on in its degradation? Then let it tell you, this heart you see into, what I wanted as I tried to do a wrong without reason, having no motive for wrongdoing but its very wrongness. The act was ugly, and that is what I loved in it. I was in love with my loss, with my own lack, and not because I loved

L1 *disarticulated]* For *dis-siliens,* "leaping apart" out of unity, see T 11.39, where Augustine was torn between different times, "disarticulated" *(dis-silui)* into them.

L8 *ready at redress]* To go with the alliterations of *vindictae aviditas.*

L10 *wander from]* The theme of wandering in his "third age," and of the Prodigal, announced in the opening of this book, is never far from Augustine's mind.

L12 *disinterested friendship]* Augustine accepted Cicero's definition (*Friendship* 6) of *amicitia:* "An agreement at the divine and human level effected by benevolence and love." See Augustine, *Answer to the Skeptics* 3.13. By this standard, not only were his cronies in the pear theft no true friends, but even his friendship with the man who dies at T 4.8 was not a true one.

L20 *hearts in order]* Psalm 63.11: "There will be praise for all who keep their hearts in order."

the lack itself. My soul was perverse, was disarticulated out of its basis in you, not seeking another thing by shameful means but seeking shame itself.

10.   Admittedly, the beauty of physical things is appealing (gold, silver, and the rest), and we sway to what touches the flesh or affects any of the senses by its fitness to them. There is a dignity in worldly respect and in the power to order others about or to subdue them (which makes us so ready at redress for wrong). Yet to gain even these good things we should not give up you, God, nor wander from your law. Life in this world has its enticements because it accommodates us to its order, patterned to beautiful (lower) things. Disinterested friendship, for instance, is a sweet linking that brings separate souls into harmony. Sin arises from this, and from things like this, only if a disordered fixation on lower goods draws us off from better and higher goods, and thus from the highest good of all, you my God, your truth, your law. For no matter how delightful these lower things are, they cannot match my God, who made them all, since he delights the just man, and is delight itself for those 'who keep their hearts in order.'

11.   When the motive for a crime is sought, none is accepted unless the eagerness to get goods of the lower sort just mentioned, or to avoid their loss, is considered a possibility. For they *are* beautiful, they *do* please, even if they must be abandoned for, or subordinated to, higher and more fulfilling goods. A murder is committed. Why? To get another man's wife or wealth, or to snatch at the necessities of life. Or for fear that someone would deprive the murderer of such things. Or from a

L4 *evil without motive*]   Sallust, *Catiline's War* 16.3: "If no motive were at hand for doing wrong, he had his gang attack and murder innocent as well as guilty passersby—in other words, to keep their hands or hearts from losing their edge for lack of practice, he was bad and brutal without motive."

L9 *exiguous family estate*]   Sallust, *Catiline's War* 5.7: "His mind grew more and more frenzied because of an exiguous family estate and a criminal record, both of which he had worsened by the designs mentioned earlier."

L14 *in fact exist*]   Another probe of the problem of evil's non-being. See Appendix, page 76.

L28 *[airy] places*]   The beauty of all physical things is inclusively catalogued in terms of the four elements, in the customary order of their dignity: fire (stars), air (the stars' places, *locis*), earth, and water.

sense of wrong burning for redress. Who murders with no motive but the mere murdering? Who would credit such a motive? Though it was said of one deranged and brutal man that he was 'evil without motive,' yet a motive was given in the same passage: 'to keep hands or hearts from losing their edge for lack of practice." Ask him, Why keep up this practice?—so that by this training in crime he could take over the city and reap honors, dominion, and wealth, escaping legal intimidation and other obstacles placed in his path by 'an exiguous family estate and a criminal record.' So even Catiline did not love his crime for its own sake but for the objects to be gained by it.

12.   But what could I, pitiful I, have found lovable in you, my robbery, my midnight deed of the sixteenth year of my life? There was no beauty in you as such, as robbery. Do you in fact exist, for me to address you? There was beauty in the pears I stole, insofar as they were made by you, the most beautiful of all things, who made all beautiful things, you the good God, and the supreme good and my true good. Still, I had plenty of pears that were better, and these I stole only to be stealing, since I threw them away once they were stolen. I dined on the crime itself, which is what I wanted to savor. If I tasted any of the pears, it was the crime that had flavor for me. At present, however, I still need to know exactly why robbery was an object of desire. As a robbery, it has no beauty of its own. It lacks not merely the [moral] beauty of fairness and foresight, or the [human] beauty of intellect and memory and sensation and animation, or the [physical] beauty of things like the stars, patterned in their [airy] places, or earth and sea, teeming with

L2 *shadowy beauty]*   The theme of the sinner hiding in shadows, broached in the first paragraph of Book Two, is kept alive.

L4 *Pride, for instance]*   In a bravura paragraph Augustine lists fourteen vices that try (unlike robbery) to pose as virtues, and he appends to each the divine quality that they mimic and distort.

L13 *transgressive knowledge]*   Augustine explains what he means by *curiositas* at T 10.55, where its principal forms are sadomasochism and occultism, which *do* mask themselves as expeditions into deeper knowledge.

L15 *Willful ignorance]*   Augustine clearly means a culpable ignorance, one that does not try to find the Lord, especially by studying Scripture *(comm.)*.

L23 *shadow of generosity]*   See "shadowy beauty", above. Also Sallust, *Catiline's War* 52.11: "Giving away someone else's belongings has become 'generosity.' "

L27 *vindicates more justly]*   Romans 12.19: "Vindication is mine, says the Lord, I will give redress."

offspring renewed by those born to fill the place of those dying—no, robbery has not even the maimed and shadowy beauty that some sins pretend to.

13. Pride, for instance, feigns loftiness (though you alone are high above all). And worldly designs aim at honor and glory (though you alone deserve to be honored and glorified eternally). Naked aggression is meant to instill awe in others (though who is more awesome than you, whose power can neither be usurped nor diminished, not at any time or anywhere, by any means or anyone). The intimacies of the sensual are meant to express love (though nothing is more intimate than your love, and nothing can be more securely loved than your truth, surpassing all shapely or shining things). Transgressive knowledge feigns a zeal for wisdom (though you alone have the deepest knowledge of everything). Willful ignorance would pass for simplicity, and dullness for innocence (though nothing can be found like your simplicity, and what could be more innocent than you, who let others punish themselves by what they do). Sloth affects to seek serenity (though where can true serenity be but in the Lord). Self-pampering would be called fullness and satisfaction (though you are fullness, endlessly replete with a delectation that never fades). Wastefulness throws over itself the shadow of generosity (though you are the most lavish provider of all good things). Stinginess wants to have many possessions (though you are everything's owner). Envy contests supremacy (though who is more supreme than you). Anger wants vindication (though who vindicates more justly than you). Cowardice recoils from any surprising or sudden

L6 *plays your unfaithful lover]* Psalm 72.27: "You destroy any who play your unfaithful lover."

L14 *in, admittedly]* *vel* is concessive (O 2.138).

L19 *flees the Lord]* Job 7.2: "As a servant, fearing his lord, courts shadow."

L21 *allured . . . allowed]* See the play on *liberet . . . liceret* in **[9]**, and Introduction, page 26.

L23 *What can I offer back]* Psalm 115.12: "What can I offer back to the Lord for all that he has offered back to me?" Augustine explains that God has "offered back" good for evil in all prior dealings with men, who are born in sin (*Explaining the Psalms* 115.4).

L25 *testimony to your name]* Psalm 53.8: "I shall testify to your name, Lord, that you are good."

L27 *dissolved my sins]* Ecclesiasticus 3.17: "As ice by balmy weather, so your sins will be melted."

menace to what it loves, and prepares for its repulse (though what can surprise you, be sudden to you, or deprive you of loved things, since you protect them entirely). Melancholy pines for lost things by which it was comforted, and wants to have them back (though you are the one who loses nothing).

14. That is how the soul 'plays your unfaithful lover,' abandoning you, seeking pure and luminous things that are not to be found except by return to you. All men mount a grotesque imitation of you when they set you at a distance in order to exalt themselves above you. Yet even in this mimicry of you they indicate that it is you, the creator of all nature, they would be, and they cannot extract themselves from that nature. So how, by the love of my own robbery, was I imitating you— in, admittedly, some grotesque and twisted way? Was it a delight in breaking your law, though only in feigned ways, where I could not openly overbear it—was I, that is, enacting a prisoner's maimed freedom, breaking rules where punishment did not reach, in a shadowy pretense at being able to do anything I want? In this I became your servant [Adam] who 'flees the Lord and courts shadow.' What rottenness is here, what living enormity, what a downward plunge into death—to be allured by what was not allowed, just because it was not allowed.

15. 'What can I offer back to the Lord' for the fact that what my memory recalls my soul no longer fears? Love I can offer back, Lord, and gratitude and 'testimony to your name that you have forgiven me' my wrong and malicious acts. I give credit to your favor and pity that you have 'dissolved my sins like melting ice.' Your grace I credit, as well, for all the wrongs I

L12 *more properly]*   Augustine has to add this, since all humans are sick with original sin and in need of *some* healing—even those (like Pelagius) who might claim to a sinless life (as compared to Augustine's).

L15 *sin's symptoms]*   The *languores* are the aftereffects of the soul's sickness Augustine has been describing, the lingering weakness, left by his sinning, that provides signs of the cure needed.

L16 *What was I seeking]*   Romans 6.21: "What were you seeking that now embarrasses you?"

L19 *was a nothing]*   The sin is, in itself, a choice for non-being.

L27 *sends light into my heart]*   Ecclesiasticus 2.10: "Love him, and light will be sent into your hearts."

L28 *divides it from the shadows]*   Genesis 1.4: "And God divided the light from the darkness." The shadow imagery associated with Adam's sin (**[14]** and Introduction, pages 21–22) is now pursued farther back in time, to the creation of light out of darkness in Genesis *(comm.).*

did not commit. Is there any crime I might *not* have committed, who could love a crime without motive? Yet that, and all else, you have forgiven, both what I did under my own initiative, and what under your leadership I did not do. What man honestly aware of his own frailty can attribute any chastity or innocence to his own control, as if he has less need to love you because he does not need your pity as much as those whose sins you forgive when they return to you? Anyone called by you, who answers your call, who avoids the sins that I am remembering and confessing, should not mock me if my illness was healed by the same physician who kept him from falling sick—or, more properly, from falling into so deep a sickness as mine. He should love you not merely as much as I do, but more, when he sees that the one who has stripped me of my sin's symptoms kept him free of such symptoms.

16. 'What was I seeking at that time, in my pitiable state, that it now shames me to recall?'—what, especially, in that robbery where nothing but the robbery was what I loved, where the robbery itself was a nothing, and I so much the more pitiful [for wanting nothing]? But there is this to be said: alone I would not have done it—I call up again my state of mind on that point—there is no way I would have done it alone. So I must have loved a partnership with my fellows in the theft. Can I say, then, that I did love something else beyond the theft? Not really, since the something else was also a nothing. For what else could that [partnership] be called in reality? (And who can help me understand this but the one 'who sends light into my heart' and 'divides it from the shadows there.') What is

L8  *reaction*]  *Affectus* is the soul's response to excitements *(perturbationes)* like fear and desire (T 10.22). So *affectus* is often translated as "emotion" or "passion." But the soul for Augustine is always active, not just receptive; so its re-*action* is what puts it in motion to respond.

L10  *Who can understand*]  Psalm 18.13: "Who can see what is wanting?"

L12  *incapable*]  Augustine was at this time the protégé of Thagaste's multi-millionaire Romanian, who was able to see genius already in the sixteen-year-old. The idea that this pampered and bookish fellow would be behind the pointless sneak-theft would not naturally occur to anyone.

L13  *go on rejecting*]  Most translators take *nolebant* (be rejecting) to mean that people would reject (condemn) the *act*. But the chortling is over the fact that people not only would not suspect Augustine and his gang but would reject the notion that they were guilty even if the suspicion arose. The imperfect tense suits this sense better, where the condemnation of the act in general would be expressed in the perfect tense.

L23  *infectious . . . affection*]  For the etymological play of *inimica . . . amicitia*.

this robbery my mind is nagged into questioning, discoursing with it, contemplating it? I could have done it, even alone, if all I wanted was the pears, to eat them. If that were the real motive, my itch to take them would have required no friction with colluding fellows to make it catch fire. But since I cared nothing for the pears, what I wanted was to commit the crime in partnership with those sharing my sin.

17. What was my reaction to this situation? Admittedly it was a low and skulking one, and I was in woeful condition to entertain it. But what, precisely, was it? 'Who can understand what is wanting?' This was a prank. We chortled inwardly to be fooling those who thought us incapable of such an act—they would stoutly go on rejecting the idea. Why then [if I were so unlikely a culprit] did I want to do what I would not have done alone? Is it because no one laughs by himself? Well, normally one does not, even though laughter does occasionally overcome isolated individuals, men with no company at all, when some truly far-fetched sight or thought strikes them. But this act was not [like that] one I would ever have done alone, never would I have done it—that is my strong recollection in your presence, my God. I would not have robbed on my own, where *what* I robbed was not alluring but *that* I robbed. I would not have robbed at all had I been robbing alone. How infectious, then, is this affection, the mind's inexplicable swerve, the way laughter and pranks become a readiness to harm, a willingness to inflict loss, without any compensating gain, no sense of a wrong being requited! Someone has but to say, Let's do it!—and feeling shame becomes one's only shame.

L8 *into my wanderings]*   The Prodigal and Exodus imagery is continued.


L10 *terrain of deprivation]*   The Prodigal succumbs to deprivation [*egestas*] at Luke 15.14. Sallust attacks the "public deprivation [*egestas*] and private indulgence" of the Late Republic in *Catiline's War* 52.22. For Augustine's treatment of his very self as a place of exile, see T 4.12: "I inhabited myself as my own inhospitable country, one I could neither remain in nor renounce." See also T 10.25: "I am a 'terrain of trouble.' "

18.   Who can untie this knot of intertwining contradictions? It is obscene, I want no thought of it, no view of it. You who are justice, your innocence both beautiful and proper, these are what I want, with candid eyes and a fullness never filled. Only with you are perfect repose and a life without turmoil. Who enters into you enters his Lord's joy where he shall know no fear and shall possess in the best way the best. Yet I slipped away from you into my wanderings, my God, my young manhood skewed off from your stability and I became my own terrain of deprivation.

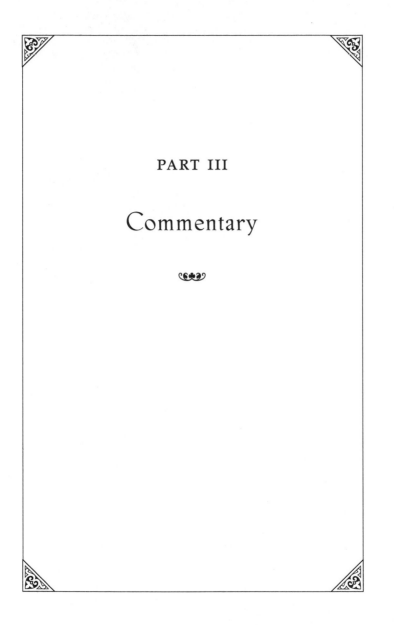

# PART III

# Commentary

**1.** For the beginning of Augustine's third age (the age of vegetation, gathered waters, and the Prodigal's wanderings), see Introduction, page 20.

**2.** For "the line [*modus*] where mind meets mind," O'Donnell (2.46–51) points to Augustine's use of *modus* as the characteristic of God the Father in his creative delineation of things. The Trinity's three persons act through *modus* and *species* and *ordo* (or their variants, *mensura* and *numerus* and *pondus*). The same sense is given the verb form of *modus* in the next paragraph—*modularetur*, "bring within boundaries." All through this opening section, the need for drawing lines and setting limits has to do with the separation of water from land on the third day of creation (Introduction, page 22).

**3.** In asking who might have marked a shoreline of marriage for his raging sea of lust, Augustine implicitly rebukes his mother, who did not counsel marriage, just restraint from married women [6]. The criticism of Monnica was explicit at T 1.18. Though he says in this paragraph that God was *beginning* to build a temple in her soul, he soon admits that she had not entirely escaped Babylon, just moved out to its periphery [8]. The irony of her failure to propose a "clear line" here is best seen by its contrast with Monnica's dream at T 3.19, where she sees her son standing with her on a "straight leveling instrument" (O 2.199–200).

Yet in the words about "sex used only for begetting," Augustine implicitly raises the suspicion that it might have been better *not* to have married at this early stage, since he could not (absent God's "gentling hand") have used sex only for procreation in marriage—as he thought a good Christian was obliged to do. See *What Good There Is in Marriage* 5.5, an implicit condemnation of himself and exoneration of his partner because of his resort to contraception after the early—and, by him, unwanted—birth of their son (T 4.2). Augustine was a Manichaean through most of this liaison, and the Manichaeans advocated the use of contraceptives.

6.  Why does Augustine say he is *clothed* with young manhood when he is clearly naked in the baths? He is anticipating a greater use of the waters gathered together on the third day of creation—his baptism, when, equally naked for total immersion, he would be "clothed in Christ Jesus" (T 8.29, citing Romans 13.14). He is naked in the baths as Adam was recognizably naked after his sin in the garden, when for the first time he had to seek a covering of leaves. The father's inspection of his body is implicitly contrasted with the *scrutinium* that all candidates for baptism underwent (Sermon 216.10–11). Several psychological readings of this passage have tried to apply the adjective *inquietum* to Augustine's penis (which is never

mentioned). The adjective modifies *adulescentia*—his life at this time was as unstable as his heart is in the famous line of T 1.1: *inquietum est cor nostrum donec requiescat in te.* As usual, the key to Augustine's meaning is theological. His father recognizes the fallen Adam in the sixteen-year-old Augustine. A different father, Bishop Ambrose, will clothe in Christ the thirty-three-year-old man, as part of a more deeply cleansing "bath." All of this is relevant, in the book devoted to Augustine's "third age," to the shaping of waters on the third day of creation.

For Monnica's attitude on his not being baptized, we must remember that baptism was often put off in Late Antiquity since there was no sacrament of penance in the later sense. One was supposed to live without major sin after being redeemed. A relapse that offended the sense of communal holiness led to excommunication. After severe acts of penance, one might be readmitted, one time; but another lapse meant permanent excommunication. This led to many a close calculation of relative dangers—could one risk dying suddenly without baptism more readily than risk a baptism that would lead to permanent excommunication and probable damnation? This passage relies on the earlier T 1.17–18:

> And you saw, Lord, how I, while still a boy, almost died from a sudden attack of chest fever—you saw, Lord and guardian, with what emotion and belief, with what reliance on my own mother and the mother of us all, your church, I begged for baptism in Christ your son. The mournful bearer of my mortal

body cared more, from her pure heart's faith in you, to deliver me into eternal life than she had to bear me into this one. She made quick arrangements for the rites of my ablution in the saving mysteries, with my testimony to you Lord Jesus, for forgiveness of my sins. Only, instantly, I recovered—so my cleansing was put off, on the assumption that I would surely be tainted as I grew up, and the taint, after such a cleansing, would be greater and more perilous. . . . Why even now is it everywhere dinned into our ears, when this or that class of men is discussed, that we should 'Let him carry on, since he is not yet baptized,' when we do not say, about physical health, 'Let him further damage his body, since he is not yet given his health.' How much better would it have been for me to be healed on the spot, so that care might be taken of myself by me and by mine, that the healing given my soul should be preserved in your preserving ways who gave it—how much better indeed. But mighty storm-waves, and many, were foreseen rolling over me after my childhood, and my mother, understanding this, preferred to commit to the waters' workings my unshaped clay rather than a self already reshaped.

This passage should be compared with the sudden death and baptism of his friend when Augustine was twenty-one (T 4.8—Appendix, page 98). By then the Augustine who had himself begged for baptism had become a man who mocked it.

9.   The reference to "young punks" is Augustine's first use of Sallust in Book Two (see also [11], [13], [18]). Sallust was one

of the four authors who made up the core curriculum of rhetorical studies in Late Antiquity (the others being Cicero, Virgil, and Terence). Augustine particularly admired (and imitated) Sallust. In an early work (*Happiness in This Life* 31) he called him "the most discriminating stylist." Writing to Saint Jerome, he called Sallust "the ablest of Latin writers" (Letter 167.6). In *The City of God* (1.5), Sallust is "the historian of preeminent truthfulness." The historian of the Late Republic was especially interesting to Africans like Augustine because one of his two historical monographs was on an African subject (*Jugurtha's War*). But Augustine's favorite of Sallust's three works was *Catiline's War*, which is cited or referred to four dozen times in *The City of God*. See Harald Hagendahl, *Augustine and the Latin Classics* (Allmquist & Wiskell, 1967), pp. 631–49.

13.   In [9] Augustine referred to Cato's speech in *Catiline's War* by Sallust, where the conspirator's youth squads are castigated (Introduction, page 9). Cato there attacks the disguising of vices under the name of virtues, which is Augustine's point here. Mocking Caesar's call for mercy toward the *adulescentuli*, Cato says (52.11–12):

> Here someone calls for "gentleness" and "mercy." That is how far we have come from calling things by their real names. Giving away someone else's belongings has become "generosity," and boldness in crime is called "courage"—to such absurdity are we reduced. Well, let men be "generous" with their

associates' goods, or "merciful" to those who rifle the public till—so long as they are not generous with our blood or merciful to "a few miscreants" who aim to destroy the law-abiding.

In his *History* (3.48.13), Sallust attacks the "slovenly misuse of terms that calls political passivity 'leisure.' " Tacitus echoed Sallust, who was his favorite Latin model, at *History* 1.37.4: "They call a base passivity 'peace.' "

On culpable ignorance as sin, see Augustine's *Unfinished Answer to Julian* 1.47:

If a blind heart were not sinful, it could not rightly be held accountable. But the "blind Pharisees" [Matthew 23.26] are rightly held accountable, and so are many others named in God's revelation. If such blindness were not the result of sin, it would not have been written: "Their malice has blinded them" [Wisdom 2.21]. And if God's judgment were not upon them, we would not read, "Let them be blinded, that they may not see, and their backs be loaded down" (Psalm 68.24).

16. What is glanced at here—the one "who sends light into my heart and divides it from the shadows there"—is spelled out at greater length later in *The Testimony* (T 13.13, 15) where the first day of creation (separation of light from darkness) is discussed:

13. In us humans, too, God has created a heaven and an earth, 'the spiritual and the fleshly parts' of our community. And our earth, before it received the shaping power of your

teaching, had 'neither radiance nor articulation.' A darkness of non-knowing was over us, for 'you chastised the sin' in us, with your 'judgment profound as an abyss.' Yet by your 'Spirit, borne over the water' we the pitiable, were not abandoned by your pity. You said: 'Be there light!' 'Repent! The reign of heaven is arriving!' Repent! 'Be there light!' And 'our souls, whirled about,' 'harked back to you from Jordan's land' and from the mountain [Christ] high as you are but low for our sake. Unhappy in our darkness, we turned to face you, and there was light, and we who once were darkness became light in the 'Lord'. . .

15.   My own faith, which you have 'kindled as a light for my steps through the night,' asks my own soul: 'Why, in your anguish, are you whirling me about? Have hope in the Lord.' His Word is 'a lamp to guide your steps.' Have hope, hold on, till night, the mother of wrongdoing, passes—'till the anger passes of that God' whose children we are, we 'who were once darkness,' and whose dark traces we still trail behind us in 'our bodies made mortal by sin,' but on whom 'day will breathe and the shadows be lifted.' Hope on, my soul, 'at morning I shall be present and shall gaze on the light,' and eternally testify to it. 'At morning I shall be present' and behold 'the rescue of my honor,' God of mine, you who shall give life even to our mortal bodies because of the Spirit that dwells in them, the Spirit of pity 'borne over our inner darkness and fluidity.' This pledge we have received in our wandering—that 'we are light even now,' so long as we hold to the expectation of rescue as sons of the light, as sons of day, no longer, as we once were, sons of the

> night and darkness. From them you alone can divide us, even in this non-final state of our knowledge, by sounding our hearts and calling our light day and their darkness night.

The words about "inner darkness and fluidity," followed immediately by a reference to the Prodigal's wandering, ties this passage back to Book Two, where Augustine's fluid state is not gathered to make firm land appear for him.

17.   The claim that one does not laugh alone is also made by Henri Bergson (*Le Rire* 1), though he goes on to qualify it, as Augustine does. One imagines oneself in company when laughing alone. The social tie is implicit in laughter, which is of its nature communicative. A comic who performs his or her act to a single person never gets the right response. An audience is required.

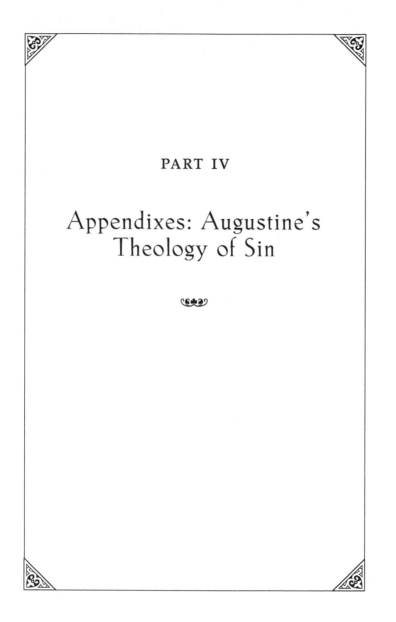

PART IV

# Appendixes: Augustine's Theology of Sin

## The Three Founding Sins

Augustine's treatment of his pear theft can be understood only against the background of Adam's sin in the garden. But that sin is, in turn, connected with—made further explicable by— two other sins. For Augustine, there were three "original sins," the second descended from the first, the third from the second. The fallen angels commit the first cosmic sin, the one that best reveals the nature of sin, since it was committed with least excuse or extenuating factors.

Tempted by the one being punished for his first sin, Adam and Eve commit the original sin for humankind. It, too, partakes of the inmost nature of sin, which is a proud substitution of oneself for God, but with a distinction between the woman's sin and the man's. Eve wants to entertain a forbidden knowledge. She is tempted by Satan, which makes her sin less "pure" than Satan's own earlier self-seduction. Adam's sin, too, is different from Eve's—he knows that he will not know more after eating the fruit, but he cannot allow Eve to suffer the consequences of her fall without his company. He acts with a "compulsion to solidarity" *(socialis necessitudo)* with her. These complications explain why Adam and Eve are redeemable but the fallen angels are not. The angels committed the purer sin, less defensible, a definitive and clearheaded rejection of God.

The third original sin is that of Cain, who founds the City of Man. He falls by resenting what God does for his brother, and is driven off to found the first city. Augustine sees in this the founding error of earthly politics, of society as built on an anti-social act. Rome, too, was founded on a brother's murder, Romulus killing Remus. The City of Man is infected from the outset with contradiction, with love of self undermining the mutual loves of community. Augustine recognizes in his own sin an extension of all these founding sins: the sin of the angels in his own greatest sin, pride (T 10.59–63), the sin of Adam in his pear theft, performed out of a "compulsion toward solidarity" with his fellow delinquents, the sin of Cain repeated in his resentment of God's treatment of his friend in Book Four of *The Testimony*.

# Appendix I: The Angels' Sin

The pear theft poses the problem of evil on the human level—how can good creatures choose evil courses. The same problem was posed even more dramatically in the biblical tale of the fallen angels. They had no bodies to pull them down, no rampant passions to choke their judgment, no maimed intellects to misrepresent their options. If sin is to be understood at all, this was the laboratory situation for testing its essence.

The problem of evil was the earliest intellectual challenge that Augustine faced. It is what made him a Manichaean. The principal attraction of that school of thought was that it seemed to explain the immense force of evil in human affairs. For a Manichaean, evil was a positive principle at war with the good. This seems to echo the psychological perception human beings have of what St. Paul called "a war in my members." But Augustine came in time to see that there can be no positive principle of evil. Since the nature of evil is negative, is destructive, is canceling, an evil with no good to prey upon would devour itself. Evil, then, has no productive capacity, only a destructive one. It has, in Aristotelian terms, no *causa efficiens* (literally *ex-faciens*, a power of *completing*). It can only have what Augustine calls, in an invented pun, a *causa deficiens* (a power of *depleting*). It is creation-in-reverse.

This saves the psychological aspect of Manichaeism without forcing one to find in evil some positive existence of its own. It is a parasite on existence leeching existence from things. The *mysterium iniquitatis* lies, for Augustine, in this paradoxical being of non-being. As he puts it in *The City of God* 12.7, "Looking for the causes of such non-being, which (as I say) does not make but unmakes, is like hoping to see darkness or hear silence." His favorite scriptural passage for this problem is Psalm 18.13, "Who can understand what is lacking?" Since humans do not have God's fullness of being, they have a lack that they can increase by turning from the source of being, uncreating themselves by partial return to the nothing they were made of.

What precisely is unmade by sin? Not the good things misused in sin. The fruit Adam ate, the pears Augustine did not eat, were not made less in their existence. A woman whose beauty is misused by lust does not become less (unless she shares in the sin). It is the sinner who contracts the self into the self, by a kind of implosion. "I was in love with my loss, with my own lack, and not because I lacked what I stole but because I loved the lack itself" **[9]**. When the sinner shrinks in his or her capacity for receiving God's light and love, other things are seen as shrunken to the sinner's measure. This is the psychological insight that we see in depictions of guilt like that of Bill Sykes in *Oliver Twist*, or the heroine in Hitchcock's *Blackmail*. Everything they see is tainted by their own act, deprived of its independent glory in their eyes. They have taken the bloom from nature, the innocence from every human contact. The world is something less for their act. They have reversed creation. This is the experiential confirmation given to Augustine's metaphysics of evil as the being of non-being. It is what Augustine describes in the following passage on the fallen angels.

## City of God 12.2–3, 6–9

2.   When we speak of the fallen angels, let no one judge that they had a nature different from that of the unfallen ones, derived from a different source, as if God had not created them also. You can stay freest from that error's blasphemy to the extent that you are attentive to God's words when he sent Moses to the Israelites. He said, "I am the I-am" [Exodus 3.14], for God is pure being, pure is-ing, and therefore unchangeable [since he would have to change to something that he was not before, and he already is all that he can be]. Things he made *are* because of him, but are not (like him) all that they can be, since they are made from nothing. Some things he made to *be* in a higher degree than others, arranging existents by the degree to which they *are*—for "existent" comes from exist-ing as "wisdom" comes from wit-ting. Older authors in our language did not have the word "existent"; it has come into use in our time to meet the lack of an equivalent for Greek *ousia*, for which existent is a word-for-word parallel. To the nature of him, therefore, who supremely is and from whom all other things are,

nothing can be opposed but what is not. Since the only contrary to what is must be a non-is, there is no existent that can be the opposite of what supremely exists, and from whom all other existents exist.

3.   When the bible calls some men "God's enemies," that is not because their nature is inimical to his, but because they bring disorder into that nature, trying to damage his rule, but just damaging themselves. These become "enemies" of God by a rebellious intent toward him, not by a damaging effect on him. How can one damage what does not change at all, much less change for the worse? So the enemies' rebellion against God harms only themselves, not God, and it does this precisely by a disintegration of their own good nature. No nature can of itself be opposed to God, but its disordering, which is bad, offends its own good nature. And since the opposite of good is evil, and God is the highest good, such disordering is aligned against him as evil against good.

We grant that God is supremely good, so a disordering of the good is opposed to him, making bad out of good. Since the one who does the disordering is also good in himself, he is opposed to his own good, and insofar as he pits his disorder against the good that is God, he directs it against himself, and there it is self-destructive. He cannot damage God, who is beyond change, unlike the changeable, degradable things he made—which are also good in themselves, as they testify by their very capacity for being harmed, since there must be a prior good for it to be capable of being disordered. For how can a thing be disordered if it has no unity, beauty, soundness, strength, or other natural good to be taken from it or diminished in it? If no such things are present, then a thing cannot be damaged by its removal, and no disordering occurs, since there cannot be any disorder that does not damage. Thus, though the unchangeable good cannot be disordered, disorder can only take place in something that is good.

It is possible for a thing to be entirely good, but not entirely evil. For even natures that are disordered with evil intent are evil only in their disordering, not in the things being disordered, which are good in their own nature. And superadded to the good that is being disordered is the punishment brought on by the disorder, since that is just, and all forms of justice are good things. It is not the good nature that is being punished but the bad intent in its disordering. Even when the disordering has the appearance of being deeply rooted in a thing's nature, because of a long course of addictive behavior, this pattern was initiated by a first disordering intent. For a disordering of intent can only occur where a rational agent judges things in terms of right and wrong.

6. The real reason for the happiness of the angels who did not fall is their connection with the one who most fully is— just as the cause of the fallen angels' woe should rightly be ascribed to their centering themselves on themselves, who lack the fullness of existence, when they gave up their centering on God, who supremely is. And what word can describe such disordering but pride? 'Pride is what gives rise to sin.' Rather than direct all their energy toward him, which would have enhanced their being by joining it with God's highest degree of being,

they achieved a lesser degree of being by substituting themselves for him. Here was the first unmaking, the first lack, the first disordering of the nature given them, a nature that did not possess the highest degree of being itself, though it had the capability for happiness derived from the highest being, along with a capability for being unhappy if they are not centered on that highest being, which makes them be less than they were before, without ceasing to be at all.

Now, if a cause that makes an evil intent should be sought, none can be found. What can produce an evil intent when it is intent that produces evil effects? The intent makes an act evil, but the intent is not itself made evil by some prior evil. A causal agent is either voluntary or involuntary. If voluntary, it must intend either good or bad. If that intent is good, only a fool would think that a good intent is what produces a bad intent. If that were so, a good intent would be the cause of sin, and what could be more absurd than that? If, on the contrary, the voluntary agent we have posited has an evil intent, I ask what could have made it evil—or, to cut short the regress [of evils causing evils], what made the original evil intent evil? No evil intent, after all, that is caused by a prior evil intent can be the cause of its own evil. An *original* evil intent can derive its evil from no other. If it does, then that prior evil is the original one.

If it is answered that nothing began the evil intent, it just always was, I ask whether the intent was that of someone intending it? If it had no intender [to be the intent of], then it never was. But if it was some intender's intent, then it was disordering and disintegrating and depriving the good nature of that intender, damaging it by depriving it of its own good. The [original] intent could not be that of the intender's evil nature, but only of a good nature capable of change for the worse by its own disordering. For an evil intent that did no damage, nor disordered itself, would not properly be an evil intent. To damage, it must have something that it *can* damage, by the removal or reduction of some good. So evil intent cannot have been always there—it had to have been preceded by some good nature which the evil intent could damage by the reduction of its good.

If we cannot say that an evil intent just always was, who gave it a beginning? Or are we forced back to the possibility that an evil intent was caused [not by an evil intender but] by something that was itself unintended? In that case, I ask whether this unintended thing is superior to the evil intent it produced, or equal to it, or inferior to it. But how can it be superior if it is something without an intent of its own—which [insofar as it is superior] would be a good intent in any case? The same holds true if it is equal to the evil intent. For if it is equal [to the good intender], it is not stronger for making it evil. That leaves us only an inferior thing without intent of its own to cause an original evil intent in the fallen angels. But any lower thing, however base and earthly, is unquestionably good insofar as it has the identity and beauty of its type and measure—and how could any such good thing [however lowly] be the positive cause of an evil intent [in angels]? How can [lowly] good produce [lofty] evil? For when some intent centers itself on a lower good by desertion of a higher good, that indeed makes it an evil intent, but not because the lower good was an evil—rather it was the recentering itself that deformed the intent. The lower good did not produce the evil intent—the intent was itself made evil by its base and disordered preference for the lower against the higher.

Suppose two men of equal physical and spiritual composition are gazing at the physical beauty of one and the same woman. One is prompted toward rape, while the other maintains the purity of his intent. What, should we say, produces an evil intent in the one and not in the other? What, more precisely, gives rise to the evil intent in the man who intends evil? It was not the physical beauty itself, since that did not have an equal effect on both men, though both were equally exposed to it. Did the man's own body cause the evil intent? Then why did it not do the same for the other? Or the man's own soul? Then why not for them both (for we have stipulated that they are the same in physical and spiritual composition)? Shall we say that the one was being secretly tempted by the devil? But even so, his own intent could become evil only by yielding to this or to some other soliciting.

What we want to know is why the response to the tempter was to intend evil. For the purpose of readiest inquiry on this line, suppose that both men are subjected to the same temptation, but only one man deliberately yields to it, while the other maintains his former condition. What sets them apart but the intent itself, one refusing, the other agreeing, to mar the good of purity? Only the intent differed, where physical and spiritual composition was the same. Both gazed on the same beauty, both underwent the same temptation. Even the most careful investigator cannot find, therefore, any [prior] factor that made the one man's intent an evil one.

If we grant that the man himself made his intent evil, what was his state prior to his evil intending but that of a creature made good by God, who is the highest good? If you have granted that only one yielded to the tempter's promptings to make an evil use of a beautiful body, while the other did not, even though both were afforded the same view of that beauty, and both had the same physical and spiritual composition before being tempted, you must ask why one man produced an intent that was evil—was it because of his nature, which was made by God, or because that nature was made out of nothing? The answer must be that the evil intent did *not* take its rise from his very nature but from the fact that his nature was created out of nothing. If the evil intent comes from his nature itself, are we not saying that a good thing gives rise to evil, even causes it, since a good creature was the cause of its own evil intent? But how can a naturally good thing, however mutable, provide from itself some prior evil that would produce, as an evil result, the evil intent?

7. Seek no more, then, for what makes but what unmakes the evil intent—not something that is, but a thing that is not. For the move from God, the highest being, to a lower being—is an unmaking of being, which is the original evil intent. Looking for the causes of such non-being, which (as I say) does not make but unmakes, is like hoping to see darkness or hear silence. We have some knowledge indeed, of darkness, and have it

only through the eyes; some knowledge of silence, and have it only through the ears; but not because of what is present to them but from what is absent. In the same way, no one should try to learn from me what I know I do not know, unless he wants me to explain how not to know what we *ought* to know can*not* be known. One can discuss or understand things knowable, not by their presence but by their absence, in a kind of knowing ignorance or ignorant knowing. When the eye, for instance, focuses its sight on physical objects, it does not see darkness until it begins *not* to see the objects. Silence, similarly, is known only by the ears—but then only when they begin *not* to hear. The intellect, too, is what sees intelligible things—but in their absence it can only know that it does not know them, for 'who understands what is lacking?' [Psalm 18.13].

8.   Of this I am certain: There can be no non-being in God, not in any time or place or manner. But things made from nothing can lack being. It is true that when they do good things (for even they can do that), they increase their making potential. But the more they unmake things by evil acts (which are futile acts), the more unmaking power they acquire. Of this, too, I am certain: since evil intent cannot arise unintentionally, it is rightly punished as a voluntary act, not a compelled one. For the unmaking motion is not down toward an evil thing, but downward in an evil way. There are no creatures that are evil in themselves, toward which they can move by their unmaking. The unmaking itself is the evil, violating its own nature—falling, in violation of the proper order in nature, from the highest being toward what has lesser being.

Avarice does not come from some disorder in gold itself, but from the man who loves it in a twisted way, preferring it to the just disposition of it. Nor does hedonism come from some disorder in dainty and luxurious objects but from a twisted love of reveling in such delights, to the damage of a self-control that fits us to spiritual dainties and incorruptible luxuries. Self-glorification comes not from disorder in the nature of human praise itself, but from a twisted desire to sacrifice the consciousness of true worth to such praise. And pride does not come from some disorder in power itself, or in any dispenser of it, but from a twisted love of substituting one's own power for a power justly held superior to it. So whoever loves any natural good in a twisted way becomes himself a good diminished by evil, and even in possession of some good loses happiness by forfeiting the higher good.

9.  So there is in nature or, as one may say, in essence, no power to make an evil intent. An evil intent arises in any spiritual being capable of change when it twists or diminishes the good nature in which it resides, and nothing can make this intent evil but some unmaking of beings by a departure from God's being, and there is nothing to make the unmaking but what is unmade.

# Appendix II: Adam's Sin

## City of God *14.10–13*

10. What bliss had they [Adam and Eve] when there were no incitements to disorient the mind, no incapacities to hamper the body—a bliss that the whole human community would have shared if the two had not committed a sin worthy of damnation, whose effects were handed on to their descendants, or if none of those descendants had committed such a sin. They would have continued in that blissful state until they filled out the number of human beings destined for happiness by acting on the benediction pronounced in the words, 'Increase and reproduce yourselves'—at which point they would have received the even greater bliss shared by the unfallen angels, with the assurance that there would be no more sin and no more dying. Humans would have lived holily, without undergoing toil, anguish, or death, in a state only to be regained now when they are resurrected from the dead with bodies not subject to decay.

11. Since God knew everything that would happen, it could not have escaped him that man would commit this sin. We must therefore write about the Holy City of God in the light of God's foreknowledge and providence, not in the light of things unknowable because they were not in God's providence.

Man could not upset God's design by his sin, as if forcing God to alter his own provisions. He knew ahead of time that man, whom he had created good, would manage to become bad— just as he knew what good he would contrive out of the bad. God is, admittedly, said to alter his provisions—in the figurative way that God is said in scripture itself to 'repent.' But this accords with the way men alter what they thought would happen or what seemed the future course of things, not to what God always knew he would be doing. He made man virtuous and free to choose—without the power to choose there would have been no virtue. The freedom to choose is God's work, since man was equipped with it by his creator. But the first act of an evil intent, since it began the whole sequence of evil, was more an un-making [de-fectus] of God's work to make something of its own, rather than a thing made in itself. That is what constitutes its evil—the will's substitution of its own working for God's work. Thus the real tree producing evil fruit was, if we may say so, man's [first] evil intent, or, more properly, man in the act of intending evil.

An evil choice, you see, is not natural but un-natural, since it is a disordering, but the person doing the disordering is natural, since nothing can exist that is not natural. The evil intent exists in a thing made out of nothing—not a thing generated from God alone, as his Word was generated, through whom everything was created. No, God made man from earth, which in turn was made from nothing, and his soul was made directly from nothing and infused in the body when man was made. Yet good prevails over evil, which is only allowed to exist so that

God may show how, in his justice and foreknowing, he can bring good out of it. Not that good cannot exist unmixed with evil—it does so in God, the true summit of being, and in all the invisible and visible beings above our darkened lower atmosphere. Evil, by contrast, cannot exist unmixed with good, since the things of which it is a disordering are in themselves natural, and by nature good. Evil, moreover, is not eliminated by removing anything natural or anything added to nature, but by the healing and reordering of the disordered and diseased. So choice is really only free when not in thrall to disorder and sin. That freedom was originally given by God, and only lost by man's own disorder, and it cannot be regained except by a new gift from the one able to give it in the first place. Truth itself informs us: 'Only if the Son frees you will you be truly free.' This is equivalent to saying: Only if the Son rescues you will you be truly rescued, for he who rescues you also frees you.

Man was living, at the outset, in a paradise both physical and spiritual—neither providing for the body's enjoyment in a way divorced from the mind's, nor providing that mind with inner perception divorced from the body's external sensation. Each was at the service of the other. But the proud angel envied this, with the same pride that had recentered him on himself instead of God, with a tyrant's special discriminating relish for ruling others instead of being ruled. As he had fallen from his own [purely] spiritual paradise, he resented man's unfallen state, and was determined to insinuate himself, with plausible contrivances, into the man's spirit, emitting his voice in the physical paradise through a serpent. Where every other animal cohabited with those two, the man and the women, and was properly subject to them while roaming harmless, the serpent—a sinuous thing that rolls on its own writhings—was an appropriate instrument for the angel. He put the serpent in spiritual thrall to his superior status as an angel, and twisted it from its proper use, making it a tool for his seductive words to the woman, beginning with her as the inferior member of the human pair, to expand his power eventually over them both.

The man, he believed, would be more skeptical, not misled himself but liable to go along with the other when she was misled. . . . In the same way, Solomon was not misled into thinking idols should be worshiped, but went along with that blasphemy when overcome by female blandishments. So we must conclude that Adam yielded to Eve in breaking God's law, not because he believed she was telling the truth, but out of a compulsion of solidarity [with her], as male to female, lone existing man to lone existing woman, human being to fellow human being, husband to wife. When the apostle [Paul] said, 'Adam was not misled, but the woman was,' he would have misspoken unless she alone believed that the serpent was telling the truth, while he refused to be rent from this special partnership [*unicum consortium*], even at the cost of joining her in sin—an act that does not free him from guilt, for this too was a knowing and conscious sin.

When the apostle says, 'he was not misled,' that does not mean 'he did not sin,' for he makes his sin clear by saying, 'Through one man sin came into the world,' and even more explicitly, later on, he speaks of 'a likeness to the collusion in crime of Adam.' He wanted us to understand that those are misled who do not think what they are doing is sinful. But Adam knew what he was doing—how else could it be true that 'Adam was not misled'? In one way, however, he may have been misled: since he had no prior experience of God's rigor, he could have made light of the offense and, without being misled precisely as his wife had been, he too was fooled, by himself, when he expected his plea to work, that 'The wife you gave me was the one who gave me the fruit that I ate.' We need nothing more to conclude that, though they were not misled together by the same error, they were convicted together in sin, tangled up together in the devil's net.

12.  Why, one may wonder, do no other sins do what this first pair's collusion did—change human nature in such a way that it is liable to the disintegrations that we witness, to death as our master, to such numerous, such powerful, such self-lashing passions that trouble and tumble us about. How different was life in paradise—though there, too, one lived in a body. No one wondering this should hold the sin a light thing or negligible just because it concerned good, and a food not evil or harmful in itself, aside from its being forbidden. God neither created nor put in that place of great happiness anything that was bad in itself. But obedience was at stake in God's command, a virtue that is the mother, as it were, and the guardian of all other virtues for any rational creature, since man prospers in proper subordination but founders when putting his own intent before that of his creator. And to refrain from this fruit alone, where all others lay about in profusion, was a rule as

easy to follow as to remember, especially since disordered passion, which would be the consequence of this sin, was not yet opposed to the command. The gravity of the sin was proportioned to the levity of its observance.

13. A covert evil preceded open disobedience. For an evil act must come from an evil intent. What could such an intent be but pride? 'All sin arises from pride.' And what is pride but the twisted yearning for one's own loftiness? What twists this loftiness is the abandonment of one's own condition, from which one should take one's identity. This is a form of self-regard, preferring to regard oneself highly even in the act of unmaking the changeless good that more deserves regard than does oneself. This unmaking was deliberate, since a continuing love of the highest good that never changes would have given light to see and fire to love where self-regard turned from the light toward a darkness, from warmth to an iciness in which Eve could believe that the serpent spoke true and Adam could ignore God's command for the sake of his wife, thinking that an act partnering him with sin could be dismissed because it partnered him with her who was his life.

What they did could not have been evil, this eating of a fruit forbidden, unless it were done by people who were evil before they ate. For 'evil fruit comes from an evil tree.' The evil of this tree could not have occurred unless it had been put to an unnatural use. The disordered intent of the user is what was unnatural. And no being could be degraded by a disordered act against nature but one made out of nothing. Everything therefore owes what it is by nature to the God who made it, but owes the unmaking of its nature to the nothingness it was made of. Though man could not entirely unmake himself, so as to go out of existence, he could, by relying on his own lesser existence, lose the greater existence he possessed when conforming to the highest being. To pull away from God and derive one's being from oneself—that is, to opt for oneself—is not to go out of existence but to draw nearer to non-existence. That is why the proud are called in scripture the ones who opt for themselves. To have a heart that strives upward is a good thing, but only when one is striving up toward God in obedience, which is the mark of the lowly, not thinking oneself able to strive up toward oneself. That is the paradox of lowliness, that it is a striving upward of the heart, while loftiness drags the heart down. It seems contradictory to say that loftiness tends down and lowliness up. But devout lowliness recognizes what is above it, and nothing is higher above it than God—so lowliness becomes lofty striving up to be under what is high, while loftiness, which is a disorder, rejects its ordering under God and falls away from him who is above all things, bringing it down to the point mentioned in scripture: 'Those raising themselves up you have thrown down.' It is not said 'those who were raised up,' as if they had been already raised before they were thrown down, but 'those raising themselves up' were thrown down. To raise oneself is, of itself, to be thrown down.

# Appendix III: Cain's Sin

The occasion for the sin Augustine spends the largest amount of time describing, after that of the pear theft, was the death of a friend. He felt that he and his friend shared a single soul, and that part of the friend therefore lived on in him, preventing him from committing suicide. Nietzsche found this ridiculous. But, then, so did Augustine. Writing his *Reconsiderations* (2.6.2) at the end of his life, he looked back on this sentence:

> When I testified to my grief at the death of a friend, claiming that we shared, in a way, a single soul between us, I said: "That explains, perhaps, my own dread of dying, lest the common soul I loved so much should entirely perish." That resembles empty rant more than real testimony, however qualified the nonsense was by my adding "perhaps."

Both Augustine and Nietzsche seem, at first, too harsh. The latter, who was a classical philologist by training, should have remembered that the idea of friends sharing a single soul is as old as Pythagoras.[1] And Augustine himself was drawing on Horace as well as on his hero, Cicero, who said (in *Duties* 1.23): "Though this may seem a stretch, the dead live on in their friends." And in *Friendship* (81–82) Cicero argued elaborately that a friend is "all but another self . . . who so mixes his soul with another that the two become, as it were, a single person."

But even though the "other self" notion is a commonplace, Augustine made it vivid in the searing description of his loss (T 4.9, 11):

> With this grief my heart was 'steeped in shadow.' Look where I would, I saw only death. My own town was a torment to me, my family home surprisingly painful. Whatever I had done with him became, without him, a source of acute suffering. My eyes were alert, everywhere, to discover him, and any place that held him not I hated for not telling me, as it had when he was absent in earlier times, that he would soon be arriving. . . . A death that could take him might, I felt, devour at once the whole human race. . . . I was astonished to see other people still living after he no longer lived whom I had loved as if he could not die. It was well said [by Horace] of a friend that he was his soul's other half. In that way I felt my soul and his to be one soul in two bodies. Which explains, perhaps, my own dread of dying, lest our common soul, so loved by me, should entirely perish.

To understand the emotional pitch of this whole episode, it is important to recognize Augustine's situation at the time. He was twenty-one years old. He had a common-law wife and a four-year-old child. He had just spent four heady years in the cosmopolitan harbor city of Carthage, and he was forced to come back to Thagaste, the hick town of his birth, in order to teach children—he owed this to the millionaire sponsor who had financed his graduate studies in Carthage, hoping to give Thagaste the intellectual boost a genius like Augustine could provide. Augustine had left behind an intellectual circle of young Manichaeans, of which he had assumed the leadership. Though he describes this circle only after fleeing back to it, its elements had clearly been assembled during his studies in Carthage. No graduate student ever felt more dizzied by new worlds opening up to him in the atmosphere of like-minded young enthusiasts:

> Other distractions more compelled my heart—conversation and laughter and mutual deferrings; shared readings of sweetly-phrased books, facetiousness alternating with things serious; heated arguing (as if with oneself) to spice our general agreement with dissent; teaching and being taught by turns; the sadness at anyone's absence, and joy at his return. Reciprocating love uses such semaphorings—a smile, a glance, a thousand winning acts—to fuse separate sparks into a single glow, no longer many souls, but one (T 4.13).

Here it is not just two people who have a single soul but a whole group. The mutual enkindling toward knowledge that Augustine felt in friendship is still there, years later, when he discusses the joys of being a Christian teacher:

> When listeners are moved as we speak, we enter into each other's reactions, the hearers speak in us and we learn in them what we were teaching. Isn't that what happens when we show others beautiful scenes which we have often gone past with a

careless glance, but which give us fresh joy as we share anyone's joy on first seeing them? And the intensity of these expe-
riences is the greater, the closer we are to each other. The more,
by the bond of love, we enter into each other's mind, the more
even old things become new for us again (*Instructing the
Young* 17).

The shared *intellectual* quest was an important part of friendship in this sense. In his snobbish days just before being baptized, Augustine had made that the sole point of being friends.
In his *Dialogue With Myself* (1.20), this exchange occurs:

*Reason:* I ask you now why you want your friends to keep on
living, even when not actually living with you.

*Augustine:* That we may together investigate our souls and
God, so that whoever discovers anything may help the others to it more readily.

*Reason:* But what if they do not join this search?

*Augustine:* I shall persuade them to.

*Reason:* What if you cannot, either because they think they already possess the truth, or that it cannot be possessed, or
because they are engaged in other business or pleasure?

*Augustine:* I shall deal with them, and they with me, as best
we can.

*Reason:* But what if their presence distracts you from your
own search? Won't you take steps, or hope to, to be rid of
them?

*Augustine:* You are right, I admit.

*Reason:* So you do not want them to live or to be with you for their own sake, but to help you find wisdom.

*Augustine:* Exactly.

Though this passage conflicts with the Ciceronian ideal of friendship (that it is not based on advantage to oneself), an ideal that Augustine endorsed emphatically, it describes the callow view of things Augustine had a decade or so before *The Testimony* was written, when he went back to Thagaste. Though he deeply loved the mother of his child (T 6.25), he did not find intellectual stimulus in her company. He did not even admit his mother could be intellectually interesting until shortly before her death—see *Order in the Universe* 2.45. O'Donnell thinks Monnica was probably illiterate (o 3.115), and Augustine's partner may have been as well. W.H.C. Frend suspects that Monnica, with a Berber name, grew up speaking the native language of Thagaste.[2] African *males* were the ones trained to read and write Latin, the "foreign" language of the empire.

It is against the backdrop of Augustine's intellectual values at the time that we must imagine the horror of his rustication at the age of twenty-one, with all the rich cultural advantages of Carthage snatched from him. One thinks of Evelyn Waugh leaving behind his golden Oxford to go teach in a dreary boys' school. Imagine Augustine's relief, then, to find at least one contemporary in Thagaste in whom he could inculcate the Manichaeism and other tastes of his friends back in the capital. He had to focus in this one soul mate all the feelings and aspirations so recently shared among many. "It was a sweet bond, fired by the eagerness of our shared studies, after I had wrenched him from the faith he was only superficially attached to (because of his youth) and brought him over to the exotic and noxious [Manichaean] beliefs my mother so lamented in me. I led him to join my wanderings, of which he was now the necessary companion" (T 4.7). He was an oasis in the intellectual desert of Thagaste.

But then the oasis turned into a mirage. When the friend was stricken by a deathly illness, his Christian family had him baptized while he was in a coma. When he revived, he was tenacious of his restored faith. Augustine tried to joke him out of it, saying his family took advantage of his weakness. The man, offended by this raillery, turned away from his mentor: "He recoiled from me with revulsion, as from a foe" (T 4.8). When, in a few days, the friend died in the comfort of the sacraments, Augustine's shock was not merely one of losing a friend to death. He was angered to find his whole intellectual system rejected. His pride was hurt. His ascendancy over the man was erased. He was stripped of the social cocoon he had been constructing for himself, the shelter to replace his lost circle in Carthage.

Augustine had no doubt tried to take his mistress away from her faith, too. He failed, since he tells us that she brought up their son in the Christian faith all through his boyhood (T 9.14), through the periods when Augustine was a Manichaean or Skeptic or Neoplatonist. But Augustine could rationalize her resistance by saying she was not educated enough to see the force of his arguments, honed in debate with his fellow intellectuals in Carthage. That a *man*, however, and one who seemed to share his values, could shake those values off so easily—that was profoundly disturbing to Augustine. It shook his confidence in his own views. He could find no comfort in the "dim illusion" *(phantasma)* of his beliefs.

> I had become a vast riddle to myself, and I asked my soul 'why, in its anguish, it was whirling me about' so thoroughly, but it had no response it could make. Had I told my soul to hope in God, it would have had no reason to comply, since the man that soul had lost was more real and important to it than the dim illusion it was being asked to hope in (T 4.9).

Augustine's tiny world was turned upside down. He was supposed to be the strong one, the leader. Yet the "disciple" was the one who showed firmness, and Augustine lost all control, all steadiness in his own creed. He became a prisoner of his grief, making it more the focus of his attention than was the lost friend (T 4.11–12).

> I was weeping bitterly, and I luxuriated in my bitterness. Miserable, I preferred the misery to my friend—though I wished it would end, I was more loath to lose it than to have lost him. . . . I was seething, sighing, crying, tossing about, unable to calm down or think clearly. . . . I held in my soul as it struggled against being held in, lacerated as it was, and blood-smeared. . . . An empty illusion, my own fiction, was my only god. When I

tried to rest my soul on the illusion, the soul slipped through
its emptiness and fell back upon me. I inhabited myself as some
alien territory, one I could neither remain in nor renounce—
for whither could my heart escape my heart, whither could I
flee from myself without myself following?

Augustine is describing what used to be called a nervous break-
down. He says that he is giving an accurate account of the
symptoms he felt. "That was my condition, so far as I can recall
it" (T 4.11). But there was one false note, he would later see. He
finds that falsehood in the claim that he may have lived on only
to keep his friend's soul alive. That contradicted the words in
which he was being ruthlessly honest with himself, admitting
that he clung to his grief and would rather give up his friend
than give up the grief. He was not just racked by sorrow, but by
complex emotions he was determined to sort out—as determined as he was to find the real motive for his theft of the
pears.

He resented his protégé's defection. He raged at a calm felt
by his erstwhile friend, a calm now spectacularly denied himself. His quotation (T 4.9) of Psalm 41.6 explains his reaction:
"Why, in your anguish, are your whirling me about?" The
Latin is an echo of what God says to Cain at Genesis 4.6: "Why,
in your anguish, is your face contorted?" In Augustine's Latin
version of the Bible, the two verses inevitably suggest each
other:

*Quare tristis es, anima mea, et quare conturbas me?*
*Quare tristis factus es, et quare concidit facies tuus?*

Augustine tells us why Cain's anguish was a sin. He was furious that God had accepted Abel's sacrifice and rejected his.

> When Cain realized that God had accepted his brother's sacrifice but not his, he should by conversion have resembled [*mutatus imitari*] his brother, not by contention have resented [*elatus aemulari*] him. Instead, in his anguish, his face was contorted. This is a sin God especially rebukes, feeling anguish over another's good fortune, especially a brother's. In fact, it was precisely to rebuke him that he asked, 'Why, in your anguish, is your face contorted?' He saw the envy that his brother Cain was feeling, and rebuked it. . . . He did this so Cain would rightly be annoyed with himself, not wrongly be annoyed with his brother. . . . For God did not send Cain away without advice that was holy, correct, and benign: 'Calm yourself, and at a second chance you will be in control [of your sacrifice].'. . . But Cain would rather eliminate than imitate his brother (*The City of God* 15.7).

This passage in Genesis was tremendously important to Augustine. When Cain flees Adam's home, the original dwelling site of man, and establishes a new city, Augustine takes that as the institution of the City of Man, opposed to the City of God, which creates all the polarities of subsequent history. It is thus, with Adam's fall, one of the two foundational sins of the entire human condition.

Augustine agreed with 1 John 3.12 that God did not accept Cain's sacrifice as a way of warning him that his life was in need of reform. But instead of taking this warning, instead of calming himself and learning from God's rebuke, Cain hugs his resentment to him, cares more for it than for his brother, luxuriates in his own bitterness. So Augustine does not learn from the return of another Christian of his hometown to the true faith, but hangs on to his own phantasma. He does not see the lesson God is trying to teach him in the difference between the faith of his friend and the anguish of his own condition.

It is true that he does not kill his friend, as Cain killed Abel. But he says he would not die for him, as Orestes would for Pylades, and he does try to kill the friend's faith, an effort he calls "my mad design," *dementia mea* (T 4.8). He cares more for his own error than for his fellow: "An empty illusion, my own fiction, was my only god." Like Cain, he has a panicky urge to flee. And he does: *Fugi de patria* (T 4.12). Cain went to found the City of Man, which Augustine often calls by its biblical symbol Babylon. Augustine flees back to his own City of Man, to Carthage, which is called Babylon in [8]. There his own will can be fortified against God's grace. "It was precisely the comfort of more friendships that eased and restored me, with whom I could continue loving some substitute for you, something made up of pretense, some way of prolonging my deception" (T 4.13). He was in a land of falsehood and he was himself that land. As Cain deserted the human family of Adam and Eve, Augustine fled responsibility to his patron's teaching post. The friend who should have been an aid to finding God was made by him a further obstacle to that quest. Where he should by conversion have resembled, he by contention resented. Other sins there would be, many of them, but they were in a sense incidental. His own founding sins were the basic sins of the human condition—the sin of Adam, the sin of Cain.

## Notes to Appendix III

1. Andrew R. Dyck, *A Commentary on Cicero, "De Officiis"* (University of Michigan Press, 1996), pp. 177–78.
2. W.H.C. Frend, *The Donatist Church* (Oxford University Press, 1952), p. 230.

‿❧❦☙‿